A to Z Picture Activities

Phonics and Vocabulary
for Emerging Readers

ant · bee · cake · dice · eleven 11
frog · gum · hen · iguana · jam
key · lips · mouse · nuts · orange
peas · queen · ring · star · turtle
up · vase · web · fox · yarn
puzzle

by Kaye Wiley and Ethel Berger

Illustrations by Ethel Berger

PRO LINGUA ASSOCIATES

Pro Lingua Associates, Publishers
P.O. Box 1348
Brattleboro, Vermont 05302 USA
Office: 802-257-7779
Orders: 800-366-4775
Email: info@ProLinguaAssociates.com
WebStore www.ProLinguaAssociates.com
SAN: 216-0579

*At Pro Lingua
our objective is to foster an approach
to learning and teaching that we call
interplay, the interaction of language
learners and teachers with their materials,
with the language and culture,
and with each other in active, creative
and productive play.*

This book was designed by Ethel Berger in collaboration with Kaye Wiley and in consultation with A. A. Burrows. It was set in Myriad Pro. Myriad was designed for Adobe in 1991 by Robert Slimbach and Carol Twombly. It is a sans serif OpenType® type, which adjusts in weight and width as the size changes. It is noted for its elegant, open geometric forms and attractive semibold and italic variations. This book was printed and bound by Gasch in Odenton, Maryland.

Printed in the United States of America

Second printing 2012

All About Me

Name: My name is _____.

Age: I am _____ years old.

Address: My address is

_____

(number)   (street)

_____

(city)   (state)   (zip code)

Family: The names of the people in my family are:

_____

_____   _____

_____   _____

Contents

A to Z Picture Activities: Phonics and Vocabulary for Emerging Readers

The Sounds of English

Sounds	**Examples of the sounds and their spellings**
A	bat, apple, acrobat
AH	bar, father, jar, octopus
AI	bait, bay, cake
AY	bite, fly, night
AW	ball, walk, saw, saucer
EE	be, beat, beet, baby
E	bet, elephant
ER	bird, burn, learn, word, fern
I	bit, give, cymbal
O	boat, rope, snow, go
OO	boot, glue, screw, tube, fruit
OU	bout, cow, cloud
OY	boy, coin
U	book, pull, hood
UH	but, above, son, umpire, under
uh	above, elephant, alligator, octopus
B	bus, bat, bubble
CH	chair, picture, catch
D	dolphin added
F	fish, offer, laugh
G	gorilla, egg
H	horse, hat
J	jump, jet, giant
K	kite, duck, queen
L	ball, bottle, medal
M	moon, hammer, comb
N	nest, runner, knock, sign
NG	sing, hanger
P	pear, pepper, map
R	robot, red, hurry
S	star, glass, center
SH	shovel, action
T	tiger, ten, better, jet
TH	the, this
th	thirty, tooth
V	van, over
W	watch, question
Y	yarn, crayon
Z	zebra, buzzard, has
ZH	pleasure

A to Z Picture Activities: Phonics and Vocabulary for Emerging Readers

Letters of the English Alphabet

A a B b C c D d E e F f
G g H h I i J j K k L l M m
N n O o P p Q q R r S s T t
U u V v W w X x Y y Z z

𝒜 𝐵 𝒞 𝒟 𝐸 𝐹 𝒢 𝐻 𝐼
𝒥 𝒦 �ℒ 𝑀 𝒩 𝒪 𝒫 𝒬 𝑅
𝒮 𝒯 𝒰 𝒱 𝒲 𝒳 𝒴 𝒵

a b c d e f g h i j k l m n
o p q r s t u v w x y z

a b c d e f g h i j k l m n o p q r s t u v w x y z

A
B
C
D
E
F
G
H
I
J
K
L
M
N
O
P
Q
R
S
T
U
V
W
X
Y
Z

A a acrobat

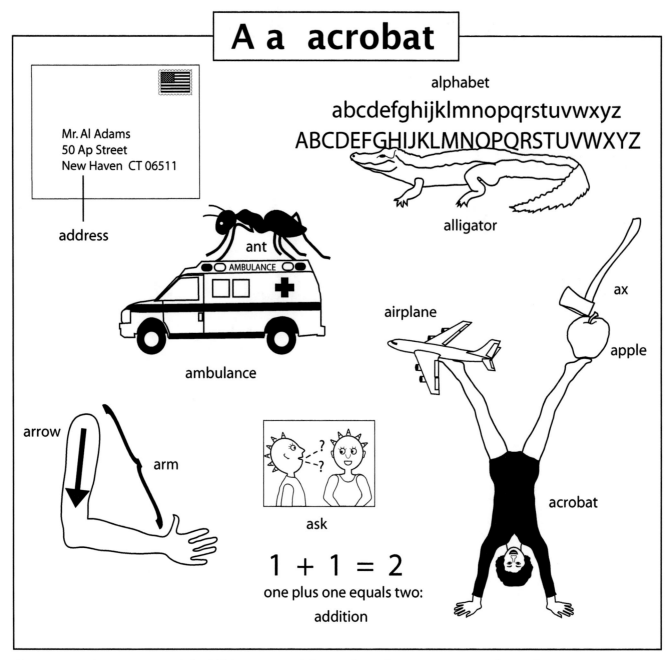

On means *in contact with*. Write a word from the picture to complete the sentence.

1. The ant is on the _____ *ambulance* _____.

2. The apple is on the _____.

3. The arrow is on the _____.

4. The alphabet is on the _____ .

Write your own sentence using words from the picture.

5. The _____ is on the _____ .

An Apple, An Ant

An is an indefinite article. We use *an* before words that start with a vowel sound to make a general statement beginning with *there is*.

Underline yes if the sentence matches the picture on p. 2. Underline no if it does not.

1. There is an apple on an ambulance.   yes   <u>no</u>

2. There is an ant on an airplane.   yes   no

3. There is an ant on an apple.   yes.   no

4. There is an ax on an apple.   yes   no

5. There is an alphabet on an arm.   yes   no

6. There is an alphabet on an alligator.   yes   no

Write the *a* or *ar* word to complete the sentence.

a. There is an _____*ant*_____ on an ambulance.
          (ant / arm)

b. There is an _____ on an acrobat.
          (alligator / airplane)

c. There is an _____ on an arm.
          (arrow / address)

Activity: Rewrite all the sentences above that match the picture on page 2.

Phonics: Short A and Ar

a

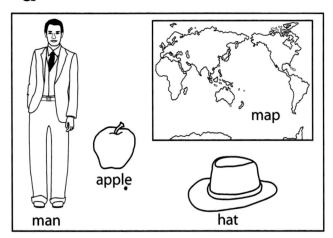

man · apple · map · hat

ar

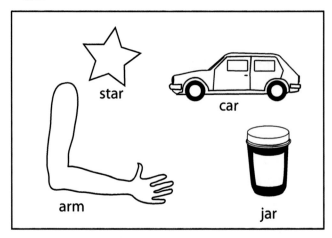

star · car · arm · jar

Short a makes the sound **/A/** as in **bat**. **Ar** makes the sound **/AH/** as in **bar**.

Complete the sentence with the **a** or **ar** word for the picture.

1. The man has a _____*hat*_____ .

2. The alligator has an _____ .

3. The acrobat has a bad _____.

4. The jar has a _____ on it.

5. The_____ has an ant on it.

6. The_____ has an arrow on it.

Phonics: Long A

a-e

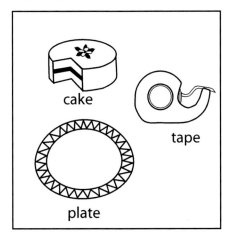

cake

tape

plate

ai

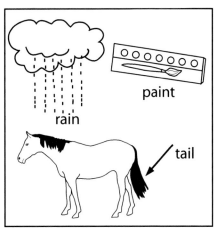

paint

rain

tail

ay

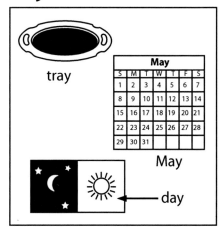

tray

May

day

Long a: *a-e*, *ai* and *ay* make the sound **/AI/**, as in **A**, B, C.

Complete the sentence with the *a-e*, *ai*, or *ay* word for the picture.

1. The apple is on the _____ *tray* _____.

2. The alligator has a _____ .

3. The _____ box has a brush in it.

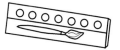

4. The _____ is very hot.

5. The ambulance is in the _____ .

6. The _____ is on the plate.

Phonics: Aw

alk, all, alt

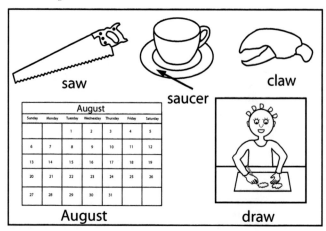

walk   salt   chalk

ball

fall

chalk

aw, au

saw   saucer   claw

August

August   draw

The letter **a** in **all**, **alk**, **alt**, **aw**, and **au** makes the sound **/AW/** as in **cough**.

Complete the sentence with the **all**, **alk**, **alt**, **aw**, or **au** word for the picture.

1. He is catching the _____ *ball* _____ .

2. A _____ can cut wood.

3. The cup is on the _____ .

4. I like to _____ pictures.

5. We _____ to school at 8:00 A.M.

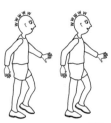

6. She likes to put _____ on her eggs.

A to Z Picture Activities: Phonics and Vocabulary for Emerging Readers

Short A, Long A, Ar, and Aw

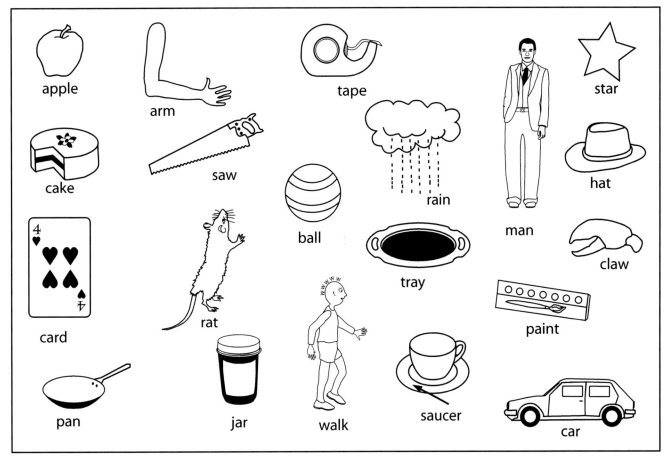

apple

arm

tape

star

cake

saw

hat

card

ball

rain

man

claw

rat

tray

paint

pan

jar

walk

saucer

car

Write the **short a**, **long a**, **ar**, or **aw** word from the picture under its sound.

short a	long a	ar	aw
apple			

Animals and the Alphabet

alligator

monkey

dog

shark

cow

horse

octopus

giraffe

tiger

elephant

lion

pig

abcdefghijklmnopqrstuvwxyz

Alphabetize the animals in the picture so they are in a-b-c order. The first letters of numbers 2-8 are given. Complete those names and add the rest.

1. **a** _____*alligator*_____   7. **l** _____

2. **c** _____   8. **m**_____

3. **d** _____   9. _____

4. **e** _____   10. _____

5. **g** _____   11. _____

6. **h** _____   12. _____

An Automobile and the Alphabet

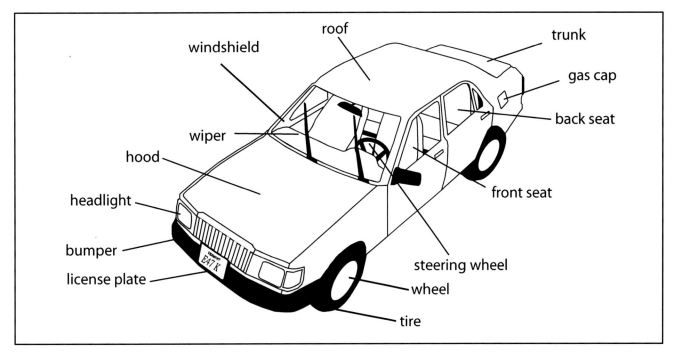

abcdefghijklmnopqrstuvwxyz

Alphabetize the parts of the automobile in the picture so that both the first and second letters are in a-b-c order. The words for 1 and 2 are given. Complete the list.

1. **b** _____ ***ba**ck seat* _____

8. _____

2. **b** _____ ***bu**mper* _____

9. _____

3. _____

10. _____

4. _____

11. _____

5. _____

12. _____

6. _____

13. _____

7. _____

14. _____

B b bus

bug

bird

branch

bear

ball

bus

bag

bed

boy

book

butterfly

bike

banana

bowl

bread

box

brush

Write a word from the picture to complete the sentence.

1. The boy is on the _____*bed*_____ .

2. The bird is on the _____ .

3. The ball is on the _____ .

4. The bag is on the _____ .

Write your own sentence using words from the picture.

5. The _____is on the _____ .

 # Big or Little?

Underline *Yes* if the sentence matches the picture on page 10.
Underline *No* if it does not.

1.	The bear is big.	<u>Yes</u>	No
2.	The bug is big.	Yes	No
3.	The bus is little.	Yes.	No,
4.	The bed is big.	Yes	No
5.	The bird is big.	Yes	No
6.	The butterfly is little.	Yes	No

Write the word that tells about the picture.

a.   The branch is _____*big*_____ .
                    (big / little)

b.   The brush is _____ .
                    (big / little)

c.   The banana is _____ .
                    (big / little)

Activity: Rewrite all the sentences above that match the picture on page 10.

Phonics: Beginning Blends

bl

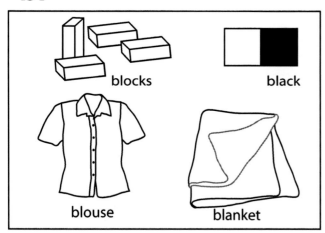

blocks

black

blouse

blanket

br

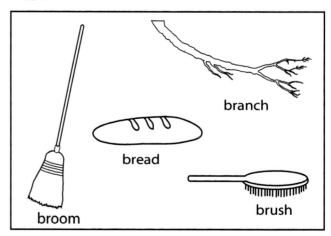

branch

bread

brush

broom

Consonant Blends: **b + l** and **b + r** form the beginning consonant sounds **/BL/** and **/BR/**.
Complete the sentence with the **bl** or **br** word for the picture.

1. The ball is by the_____*blocks*_____.

2. The_____ is on the bed.

3. The_____ is on the bag.

4. The black bird is on the _____ .

5. The_____ is in the box.

6. The bug is on the_____ .

Parts of the Body

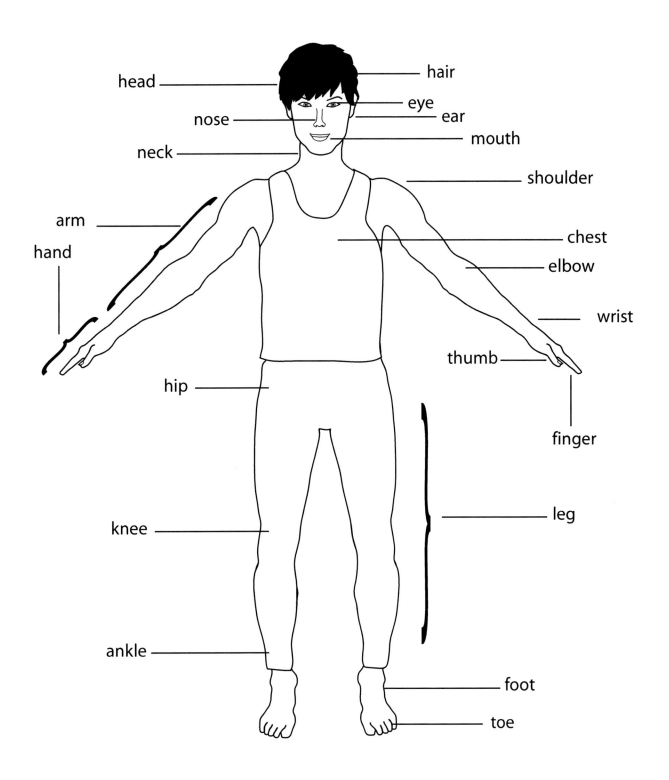

head — hair

eye

nose — ear

mouth

neck — shoulder

arm — chest

hand — elbow

wrist

thumb

hip — finger

knee — leg

ankle — foot

toe

Play the game "Simon Says" with a partner to practice the words in the picture.

C c catch

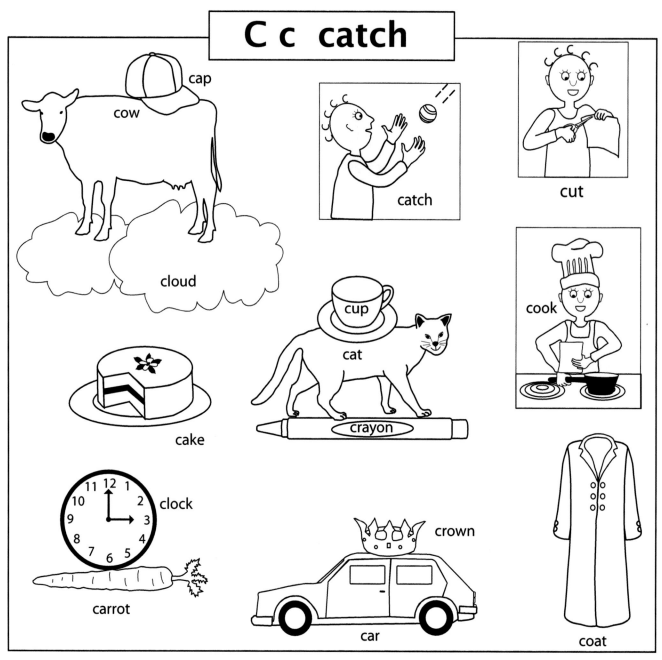

cap

cow

catch

cut

cloud

cup

cat

cook

cake

crayon

11 12 1
10   2
9   3
8   4
7 6 5

clock

crown

carrot

car

coat

Write a word from the picture to complete the sentence.

1. The cap is on the _____ cow _____.

2. The cup is on the _____.

3. The cat is on the _____.

4. The clock is on the _____.

Write your own sentence using words from the picture.

5. The_____ is on the _____ .

Can you?

Underline *Yes, I can* if you can do the action shown in the picture on page 14. Underline *No, I can't* if you can't do it.

1. Can you catch a ball?   Yes, I can.   No, I can't.

2. Can you cut paper?   Yes, I can.   No, I can't.

3. Can you cook?   Yes, I can.   No, I can't.

4. Can you catch a butterfly?   Yes, I can.   No, I can't.

5. Can you cut carrots?   Yes, I can.   No, I can't.

6. Can you catch a cloud?   Yes, I can.   No, I can't.

Write *can* or *can't* to make a true sentence.

a. I_____can_____ read a book.
    (can / can't)

b. I_____ ride a bike.
    (can / can't)

c. I_____ cut bread.
    (can / can't)

Activity: Ask a partner questions starting with *Can you....?*

Phonics: Soft C and Ch

soft c

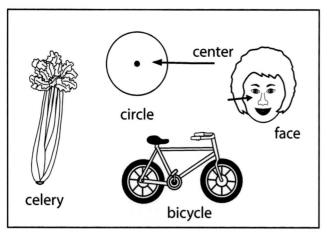

center

circle

face

celery

bicycle

ch

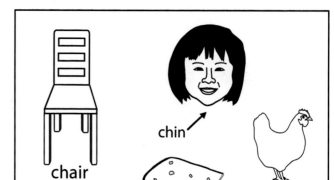

chair

chin

cheese

chicken

C makes the sound **/S/** when followed by **-e, -i,** or **-y.**

C + h makes the sound **/CH/** as in **chair.**

Complete the sentence with the **soft c** or **ch** word for the picture.

1. The _____*circle*_____ has a C in the center.

2. The chair has a _____ on it.

3. The _____ has a big chin.

4. The bag is on the _____ .

5. The tray has _____ on it.

6. The carrot is by the_____ .

A to Z Picture Activities: Phonics and Vocabulary for Emerging Readers

Colors

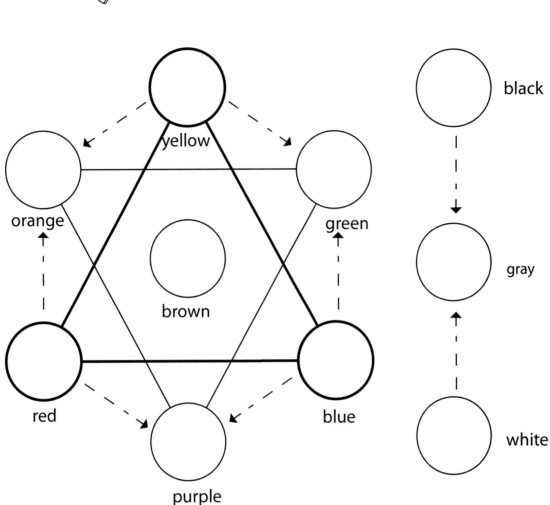

yellow

orange

green

brown

red

blue

purple

black

gray

white

1: Look at the color chart on the back cover. Use a crayon or marker to fill in each circle with the matching color.

2: Mixing colors: Follow the arrow from two dark-lined circles to the one between them. Write the name of this mixed-color circle.

a. Blue and yellow make _____*green*_____ .

b. Blue and red make _____ .

c. Red and yellow make _____ .

Counting

1	one	14	fourteen	27	twenty-seven	
2	two	15	fifteen	28	twenty-eight	
3	three	16	sixteen	29	twenty-nine	
4	four	17	seventeen	30	thirty	
5	five	18	eighteen	40	forty	
6	six	19	nineteen	50	fifty	
7	seven	20	twenty	60	sixty	
8	eight	21	twenty-one	70	seventy	
9	nine	22	twenty-two	80	eighty	
10	ten	23	twenty-three	90	ninety	
11	eleven	24	twenty-four	100	one hundred	
12	twelve	25	twenty-five	1000	one thousand	
13	thirteen	26	twenty-six	1,000,000	one million	

Write the word for each number:

16 _____*sixteen*_____   33 _____

24 _____   11 _____

70 _____   200 _____

85 _____   109 _____

Activity: Ask a partner to write other numbers as you read them from the list.

Clothes

Write about the clothes you are wearing today. Tell the color and name of each item.

I am wearing _____   *shoes*_____ .
                        (color)   (item of clothing)

I am wearing _____   _____ .
                        (color)   (item of clothing)

I am wearing _____   _____ .
                        (color)   (item of clothing)

Activity: Tell a friend what clothes you are wearing today. What color are they?

Classroom

Write the names of eight things in your classroom.

1. _____*chair*_____

2. _____

3. _____

4. _____

5. _____

6. _____

7. _____

8. _____

Activity: Draw a picture or map of your classroom. Label each thing you draw.

A to Z Picture Activities: Phonics and Vocabulary for Emerging Readers

Classroom Items

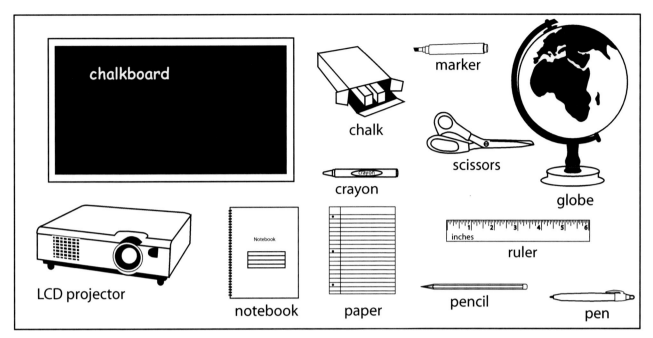

chalkboard

marker

chalk

scissors

globe

crayon

LCD projector

Notebook

notebook

paper

ruler

pencil

pen

How many of these things are in your classroom?

If there is just one of these things, underline *there is*. Write a complete sentence beginning with *There is*.

If there are more than one (or zero) of these things, underline *there are*. Write a complete sentence beginning with *There are*.

1.   How many clocks are in your classroom?

   <u>There is</u> / there are   _____*There is one clock.*_____

2.   How many chalkboards are in your classroom?

   There is / there are   _____.

3.   How many rulers are in your classroom?

   There is / there are   _____.

Activity: Make a list of all the things in your classroom.

   How many are there of each thing? Write the number beside each name.

D d dolphin

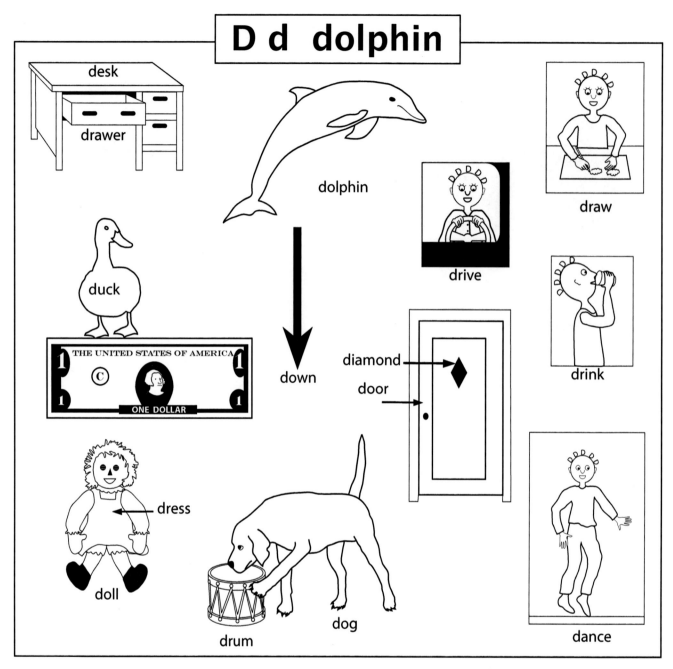

desk

drawer

duck

THE UNITED STATES OF AMERICA
ONE DOLLAR

dolphin

down

drive

diamond

door

draw

drink

dress

doll

drum

dog

dance

Write a word from the picture to complete the sentence.

1. The desk has a _____ *drawer* _____ .

2. The duck has a _____ .

3. The doll has a _____ .

4. The door has a _____ .

Write your own sentence using words from the picture.

5. The _____ is on the _____ .

A to Z Picture Activities: Phonics and Vocabulary for Emerging Readers

Do you like . . . ?

Underline *Yes, I do* if you like the thing or action shown in the picture on page 22.
Underline *No, I don't* if you do not like it.

1. Do you like dolphins?   Yes, I do.   No, I don't.

2. Do you like dogs?   Yes, I do.   No, I don't.

3. Do you like drums?   Yes, I do.   No, I don't.

4. Do you like to dance?   Yes, I do.   No, I don't.

5. Do you like to draw pictures?   Yes, I do.   No, I don't.

6. Do you like to drink milk?   Yes, I do.   No, I don't.

Write *like* or *don't like* to make a true sentence.

a.   I_____*like*_____ cake.
          (like / don't like)

b.   I_____ cats.
          (like / don't like)

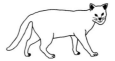

c.   I_____ to cook.
          (like / don't like)

Activity: Ask a partner questions starting with   *Do you like....?*

Phonics: Ending Blends

nd, nk, mp, sk, st, lk, lt, ft

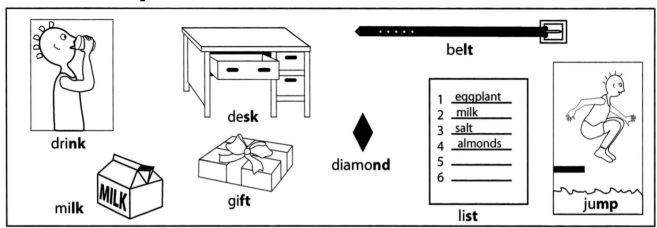

Ending Blends: When consonants like **nd**, **nk**, **sk**, **st**, **lk**, **lt**, **mp**, or **ft** come at the end of a word, they are called ending blends.

Complete the sentence with the word for the picture. Notice the ending blend.

1. The duck is on the _____*desk*_____ .

2. I like to _____ milk.

3. The _____ is black.

4. The boy has a big _____ .

5. The _____ is on the door.

6. He likes to _____ into the water.

A to Z Picture Activities: Phonics and Vocabulary for Emerging Readers

Days and Dates

December

Sunday	Monday	Tuesday	Wednesday	Thursday	Friday	Saturday
		1	2	3	4	5
6	7	8	9	10	11	12
13 Full Moon	14	15	16	17	18	19
20	21	22 Hanukkah begins	23	24	25 Christmas	26 Kwanzaa begins
27	28	29	30	31 New Year's Eve		

Write the name of the day that finishes each sentence.

1. December 9 is a _____ *Wednesday* _____ .

2. December 14 is a _____ .

3. Christmas is on a _____ .

4. New Year's Eve is on a _____ .

5. Hanukkah begins on a _____ .

6. The full moon is on a _____ .

7. December 19 is a _____ .

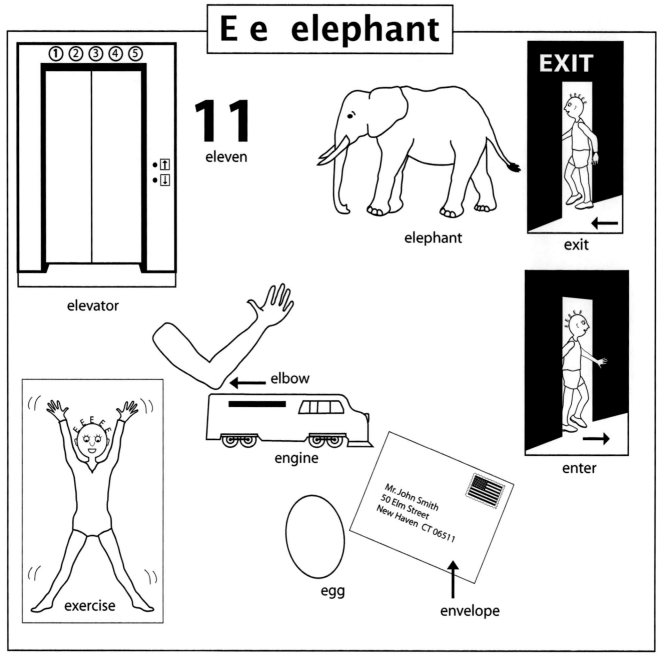

E e elephant

elevator

11 eleven

elephant

EXIT

exit

elbow

engine

enter

exercise

egg

Mr. John Smith
50 Elm Street
New Haven CT 06511

envelope

Near means *close to*. Write a word from the picture to complete the sentence.

1. The egg is near the _____*envelope*_____ .

2. The elephant is near the _____ .

3. The number eleven is near the _____ .

4. The elbow is near the _____ .

Write your own sentence using words from the picture.

5. The_____ is near the _____ .

A to Z Picture Activities: Phonics and Vocabulary for Emerging Readers

Can an elephant . . . ?

Underline *Yes,* if the subject can do the action.
Underline *No,* if it can't.

1. Can an elephant drive a car?   Yes   <u>No</u>

2. Can an acrobat exercise?   Yes   No

3. Can an engine dance?   Yes.   No,

4. Can a boy enter an elevator?   Yes   No

5. Can an elephant cook an egg?   Yes   No

6. Can an envelope catch a ball?   Yes   No

Write the word to match the picture.

a.   An _____*elephant*_____ is a big animal.

b.   An _____ is part of an arm.

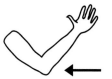

c.   The _____ has an address on it.

Mr. John Smith
50 Elm Street
New Haven CT 06511

Activity: Write four new sentences using words that start with *E.*
             Read the sentences you wrote to a partner.

Phonics: Short E and Er

e

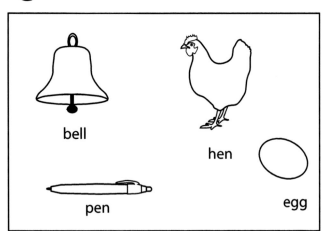

bell

hen

pen

egg

er

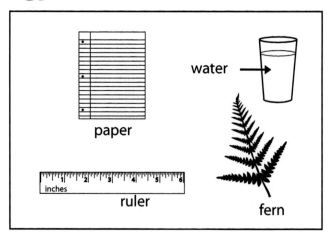

paper

water

ruler

fern

Short e makes the sound **/E/** as in **bet**. **Er** makes the sound **/ER/** as in **bird**.

Complete the sentence with the **e** or **er** word for the picture.

1. The hen has an _____ *egg* _____ .

2. The elephant has a _____ .

3. The_____ is near the paper.

4. The dog is by the_____ .

5. The glass of_____is on the tray.

6. The _____ is on the envelope.

A to Z Picture Activities: Phonics and Vocabulary for Emerging Readers

Phonics: Long E

ea

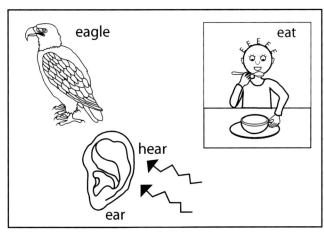

ee

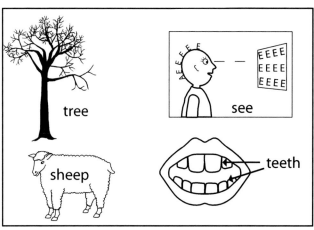

Long E: *ea* and *ee* make the sound **/EE/**.

Complete the sentence with the **ea** or **ee** word for the picture.

1. An _____*eagle*_____ is a big bird.

2. I like to _____ cereal.

3. I _____ the letter E.

4. A _____ has branches on it.

5. I hear with my _____.

6. The alligator has big _____.

Eating Out

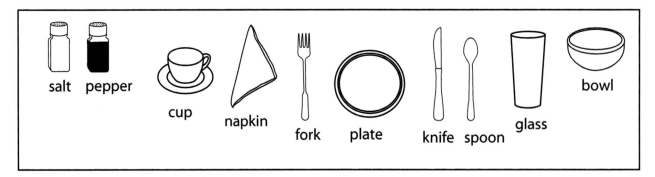

salt   pepper   cup   napkin   fork   plate   knife   spoon   glass   bowl

Write the names of food you like to eat for dinner.
You may write other foods besides those shown.

Dinner

Main Dishes

chicken   fish

steak   spaghetti

Side Dishes

rice   potato

salad   green beans

Desserts

ice cream   pie

Drinks

milk   juice

For dinner I like to eat/drink…

Main Dish:

_____
chicken
or

_____

Side Dishes:

_____
and

_____

Dessert:

_____

Drink:

_____

I like to eat . . .

Write the names of food you like to eat for breakfast and lunch.
You may write other foods besides those shown.

For breakfast I like to eat / drink...

_____

_____

_____

_____

_____

For lunch I like to eat / drink...

_____

_____

_____

_____

_____

_____

F f fish

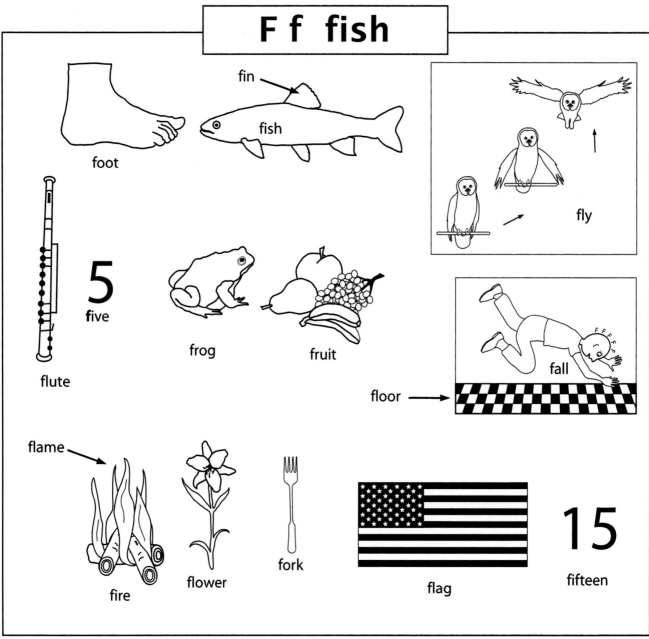

Beside means *next to*. Write a word from the picture to complete the sentence.

1. The foot is beside the _____ *fish* _____ .

2. The fire is beside the _____ .

3. The number five is beside the _____ .

4. The frog is beside the _____ .

Write your own sentence using words from the picture.

5. The _____ is beside the _____ .

A to Z Picture Activities: Phonics and Vocabulary for Emerging Readers

Flying

A verb is a word that shows action. The ending *ing* added to a verb means the action is happening now, at the present time.

Write the verb plus *ing* on the line to match the picture. Look at pages 14, 22, 26, and 32.

1. The bird is _____*flying*_____ .
   (flying, cooking)

2. The man is _____ .
   (driving, falling)

3. He is _____ a ball.
   (catching, cutting)

4. She is _____ .
   (drawing, drinking)

5. The boy is _____ .
   (dancing, driving)

6. She is _____ .
   (eating, exercising)

Activity: Rewrite all the sentences above with the verbs you chose.

Phonics: Ph and Gh

ph

phone

elephant

abcdefghijklmnopqrstuvwxyz

alphabet

gh

cough

laugh

Ph and *gh* also make the sound /**F**/ as in **fish**.

Complete the sentence with the *ph* or *gh* word for the picture.

1. He is sick and has a bad _____ *cough* _____ .

2. The _____ is on the fish.

abcdefghijklmnopqrstuvwxyz

3. The _____ has a big five on it.

4. The flower is by the _____ .

5. I have fun and _____ with my friend.

6. P, H, and G are letters in the _____ . abcdef**gh**ijklmno**p**qrstuvwxyz

Family Tree

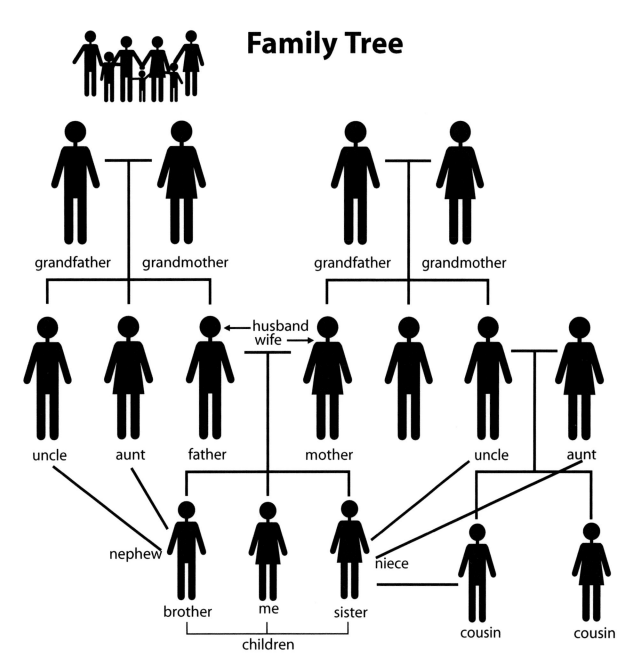

grandfather grandmother grandfather grandmother

husband
wife

uncle aunt father mother uncle aunt

nephew

niece

brother me sister cousin cousin

children

Circle the words of the family member who live in your home.

I live with my: (mother) father sister/sisters

brother/brothers grandmother grandfather

aunt uncle cousin/cousins niece

nephew wife husband children

F

My Family Tree

A family tree can be a list of names. Write the first names of the people in your family. Write the names of the older people first. List their relationship to you if you know it.

The oldest person in my family:

_____   _____*grandmother*_____
                (first name)   (family relationship)

_____   _____*mother*_____

_____   _____

_____   _____

_____   _____

Other people in my family:

_____   _____

_____   _____

_____   _____

_____   _____

Fruit

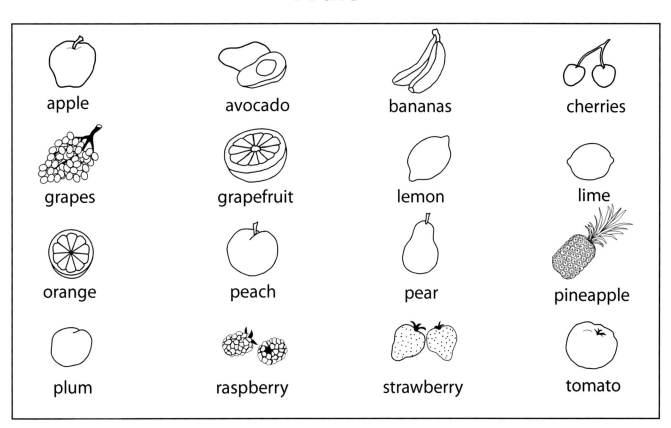

apple · avocado · bananas · cherries

grapes · grapefruit · lemon · lime

orange · peach · pear · pineapple

plum · raspberry · strawberry · tomato

F

Fruits and Colors

Put an X by the color (or colors) of these fruits. If you are not sure, look at the color chart on the back cover.

Fruits	red	green	yellow	purple	orange
apple	x	x			
avocado					
banana					
cherries					
grapes					
lemon					
grapefruit					
pear					
strawberry					

Face

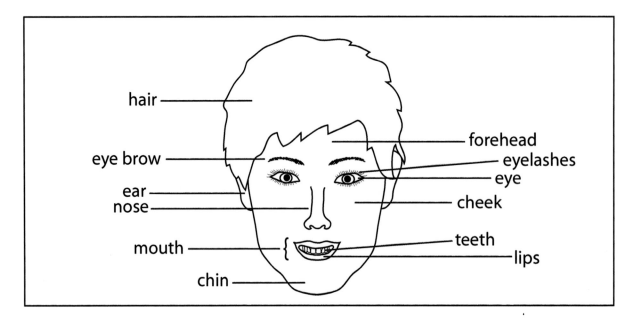

hair

forehead

eye brow

eyelashes

eye

ear

nose

cheek

mouth

teeth

lips

chin

Alien Face From   Outer Space

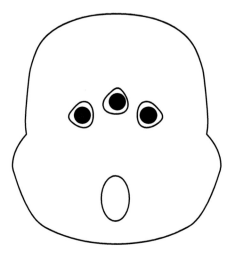

Activity: Finish this face. Write about the face from outer space on the lines below.

1. This face has three _____.

2. This face has one _____.

3. I added two big _____.

4. I added _____

_____

_____.

Feelings

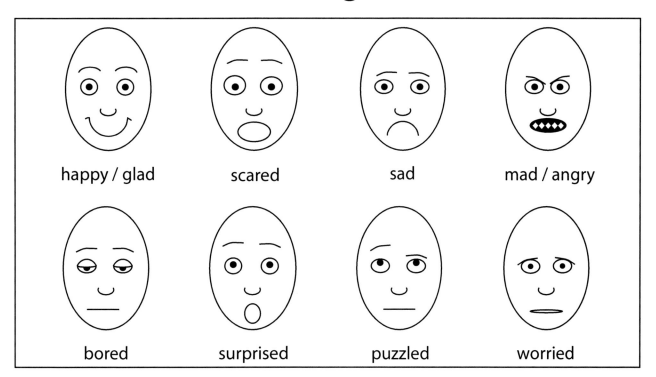

happy / glad   scared   sad   mad / angry

bored   surprised   puzzled   worried

Tell about your own feelings. Write a word from one of the pictures on the line.

1. I feel _____ *sad* _____ when my friend says goodbye.

2. I feel _____ at my birthday party.

3. I feel _____ when when someone jumps out at me.

4. I feel _____ when I don't know the answer to a problem.

5. I feel _____ when I am alone at night.

6. I feel _____ when I have nothing to do.

Write your own sentence about a different feeling.

7. I feel _____ when _____.

G g gorilla

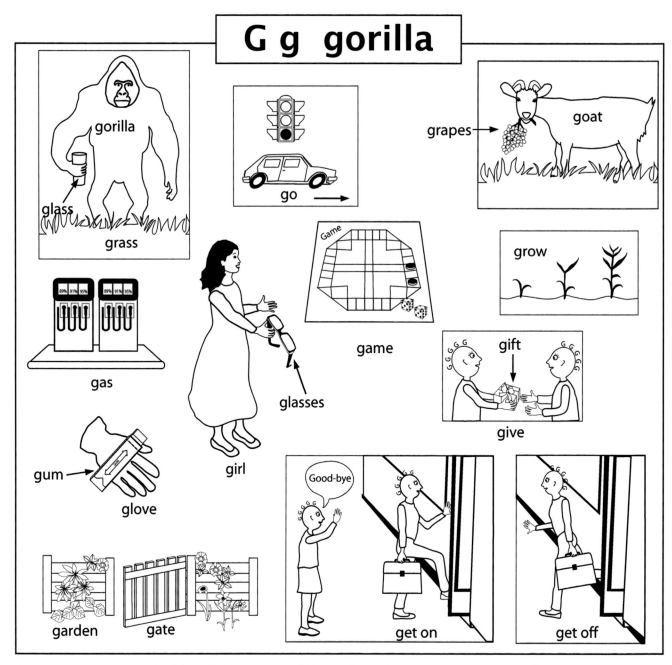

In means surrounded by. Write a word from the picture to complete the sentence.

1. The gate is in the _____ *garden* _____ .

2. The goat has _____ in his mouth.

3. The girl has _____ in her hand.

4. The gorilla is in the _____ .

Write your own sentence using words from the picture.

5. The _____ .

Giving

Write the verb plus *ing* on the line to match the picture. Look at pages 22, 29, and 40.

1. He is _____*giving*_____ a gift to his friend.
   (giving, cooking)

2. The car is_____ fast.
   (going, growing)

3. The plant is_____ in the sun.
   (giving, growing)

4. She is_____ the bus.
   (getting off, getting on)

5. The goat is_____ grapes.
   (eating, cooking)

6. She is_____ from a glass.
   (flying, drinking)

Activity: Rewrite all the sentences above with the verbs you chose.
   Write six more sentences using different verbs. Read the
   sentences you wrote to a partner.

Phonics: Soft G and NG

soft g

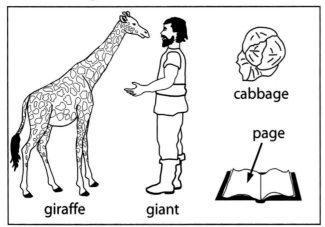

giraffe   giant   cabbage   page

ng

hanger   song   ring   sing

G usually makes the **/J/** sound when followed by **-e** (especially **silent e**), **-i**, or **-y**. This is called a **soft g**. **/NG/** is a sound that follows a vowel in words like **ring** and **song**.

Complete the sentence with the **soft g** or **ng** word for the picture.

1. The _____ *giraffe* _____ has a long neck.

2. A _____ is a round, leafy vegetable.

3. She has a _____ on her hand.

4. The _____ is as big as the tree.

5. He likes to _____ that song.

6. A _____ is part of a book.

Grains and Groceries

Grains: These grain foods come from the seeds of plants.

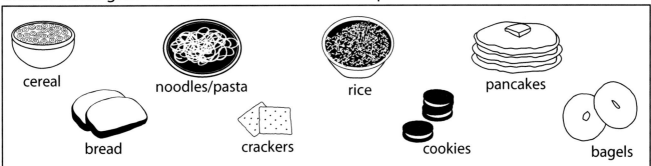

cereal
noodles/pasta
rice
pancakes
bread
crackers
cookies
bagels

Groceries: Grocery stores have other packaged foods, like these.

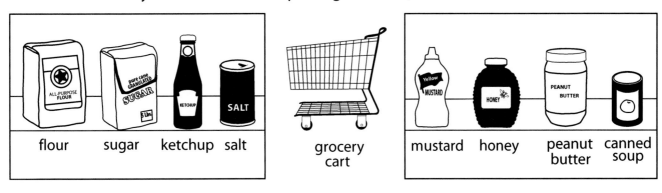

ALL-PURPOSE FLOUR
pure cane GRANULATED SUGAR
5 Lbs.
KETCHUP
SALT
Yellow MUSTARD
HONEY
PEANUT BUTTER
flour
sugar
ketchup
salt
grocery cart
mustard
honey
peanut butter
canned soup

G

Write the names of foods you like and don't like. You can list any foods.

I like to eat ...	I don't like to eat ...
cookies	

H h horse

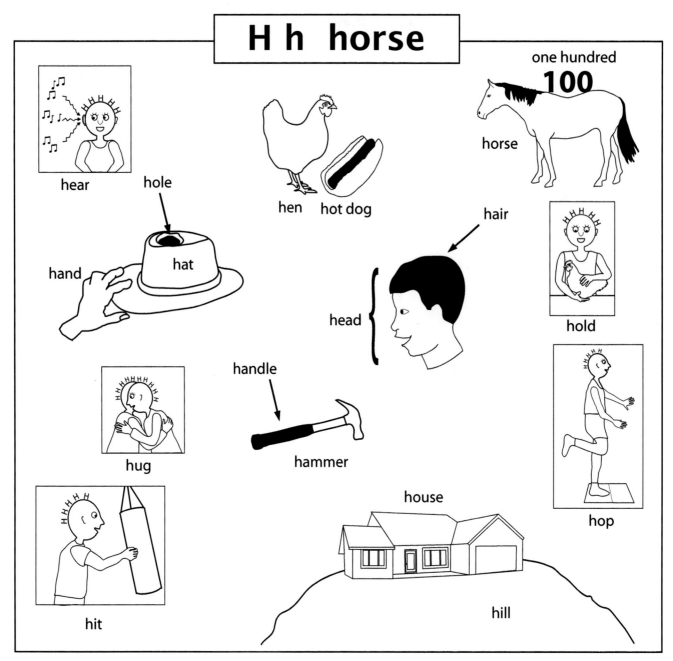

one hundred
100
horse

hear

hole

hen hot dog

hat

hand

hair

head

hold

handle

hammer

hug

hop

house

hit

hill

Write a word from the picture to complete the sentence.

1. The _____ *hat* _____ has a hole in it.

2. The house is on the_____ .

3. The boy has black _____ on his head.

4. The hot dog is near the_____ .

Write your own sentence using words from the picture.

5. The _____ .

Have / Has

The verb *have* in the simple present tense changes to *has* after *he, she,* or *it*.

Have	
singular	*plural*
I **have**	we **have**
you **have**	you **have**
he, she, it **has**	they **have**

Use the chart above to complete the sentences.

1. A hammer is a tool. It _____ **has** _____ a handle.
       (has/have)

2. Horses are big. They_____ four legs.
                    (has/have)

3. We_____ a TV in our new house.
       (has/have)

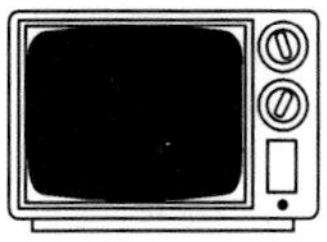

4. She_____ a hen in her hands.
       (has/have)

5. I _____ a hole in my shoe.
       (has/have)

6. You_____ my hat in your hand.
       (has/have)

Phonics: Digraphs Sh, Th, and Wh

sh

shirt · shoe · shark

th

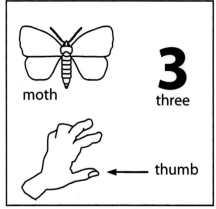

moth · **3** three · thumb

wh

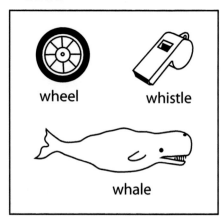

wheel · whistle · whale

Sh makes the sound **/SH/** at the end of the word **dish**.

Th makes the sound **/th/** at the end of the word **teeth**. It also makes the sound /TH/ in the word ***the***.

Wh makes the sound **/HW/** at the beginning of the word ***white***.

Complete the sentence with the *sh*, *th* or *wh* word for the picture.

1. The _____*moth*_____ is flying near the lamp.

2. A _____ has big teeth.

3. My hand has four fingers and a _____ .

4. A _____ is a mammal, not a fish.

5. One _____ is off the car.

6. I hear the sound of a _____ .

A to Z Picture Activities: Phonics and Vocabulary for Emerging Readers

H

House/ Apartment

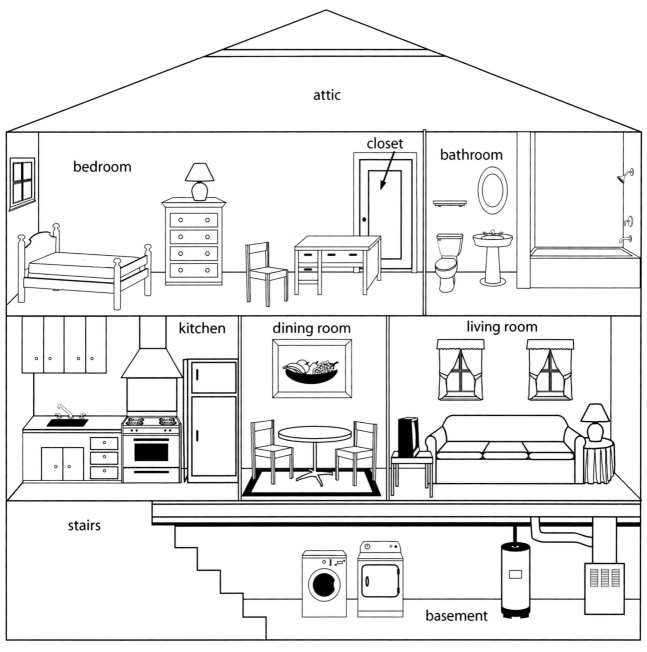

attic

closet

bedroom

bathroom

kitchen   dining room   living room

stairs

basement

Activity: Write about the place where you live.

I live in _____ .

(a house, an apartment, a condo, another kind of home)

It has _____

_____

_____

Household Items

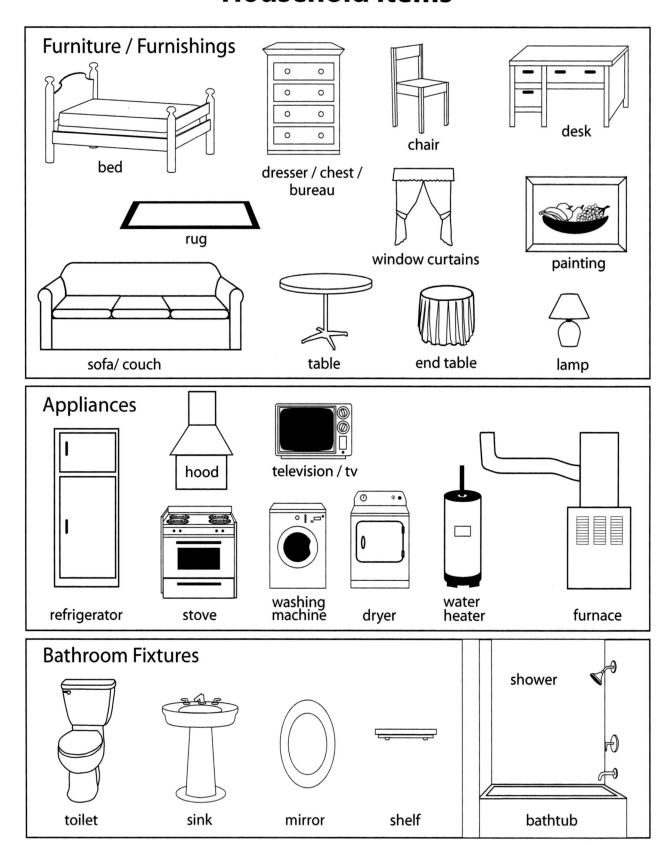

Furniture / Furnishings

bed

dresser / chest / bureau

chair

desk

rug

window curtains

painting

sofa/ couch

table

end table

lamp

Appliances

hood

television / tv

refrigerator

stove

washing machine

dryer

water heater

furnace

Bathroom Fixtures

shower

toilet

sink

mirror

shelf

bathtub

Activity: Tell a partner about the household items you have.

A to Z Picture Activities: Phonics and Vocabulary for Emerging Readers

Holiday Symbols

October 31st: **Halloween** jack-o-lantern	February 14th: **Valentine's Day** heart
4th Thursday in November: **Thanksgiving** turkey	March 17th: **St. Patrick's Day** shamrock
December 25th: **Christmas** Christmas tree	Mid-spring: **Easter** Easter basket
Mid-December: **Hanukkah** menorah	July 4th: **Independence Day** American flag

Write about your favorite holiday. You may choose any holiday.

My favorite holiday is _____

because _____

_____

_____

I i igloo

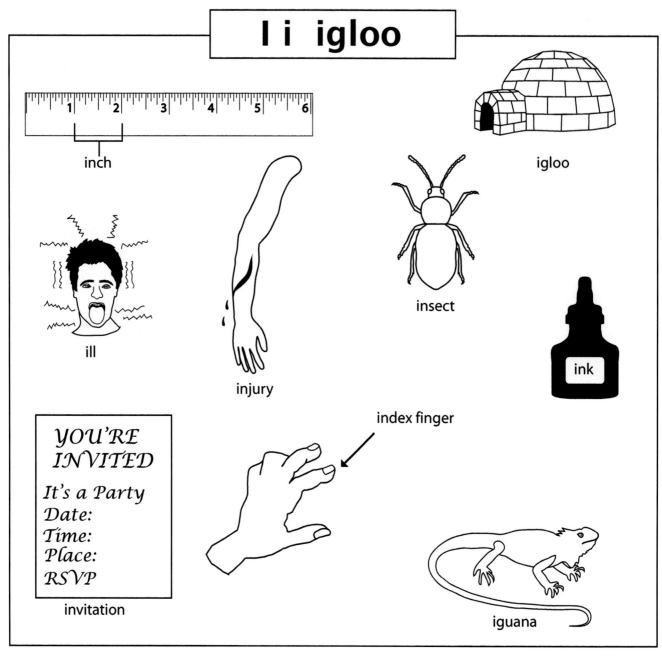

inch

igloo

insect

ink

ill

injury

index finger

YOU'RE INVITED

It's a Party
Date:
Time:
Place:
RSVP

invitation

iguana

Write a word from the picture to complete the sentence.

1. He has a bad _____ *injury* _____ on his arm.

2. An _____ is a bug with six legs.

3. An _____ has a long tail and short legs.

4. An _____ is a house made of ice blocks.

Write your own sentence using words from the picture.

5. The _____ .

Is it ... ?

To make a question with the verb *to be* we put the verb first.

to be - *question* form	
singular	*plural*
am I?	**are** we?
are you?	**are** you?
is he, **is** she, **is** it?	**are** they?

Use the chart above to complete these questions.

1. _____*Is it*_____ a flying insect?
   (Is it / Are it)

2. _____ ill with a fever?
   (Is he / Are he)

3. _____ iguanas?
   (Am they / Are they)

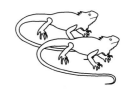

4. _____ invited to the party?
   (Are you / Is you)

5. _____ pointing with my index finger?
   (Is I / Am I)

6. _____ a bad injury?
   (Are it / Is it)

Activity: Use the chart to ask a partner your own questions.

Phonics: Short I and Ir

i

inch

fish

kiss

sit

ir

girl

shirt

bird

skirt

Short i makes the sound **/I/** as in **bit**. **Ir** makes the sound **/ER/** as in **bird**.

Complete the sentence with the **i** or **ir** word for the picture.

1. The insect is one _____*inch*_____ long.

2. The _____ has flowers on it.

3. The _____ is on the branch.

4. The fork is by the _____.

5. I _____ in a chair at school.

6. There is black ink on the_____ .

A to Z Picture Activities: Phonics and Vocabulary for Emerging Readers

Phonics: Long I

i-e

y
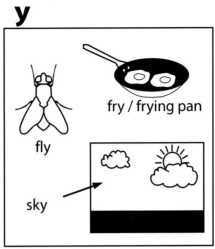

igh
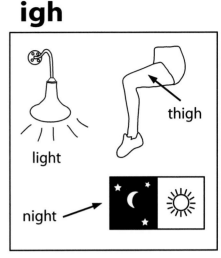

Long I: *i-e*, *y,* and *igh* make the sound **/AY/** as in the name for the letter *i*.

Complete the sentence with the *i-e*, *y*, or *igh* word for the picture.

1. I have _____*ice*_____ in my glass of water.

2. There is a light on my _____ .

3. A _____ is a kind of insect.

4. She has an injury on her _____ .

5. He likes to _____ at night.

6. The _____ is blue on a nice day.

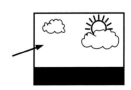

Illness and Injuries

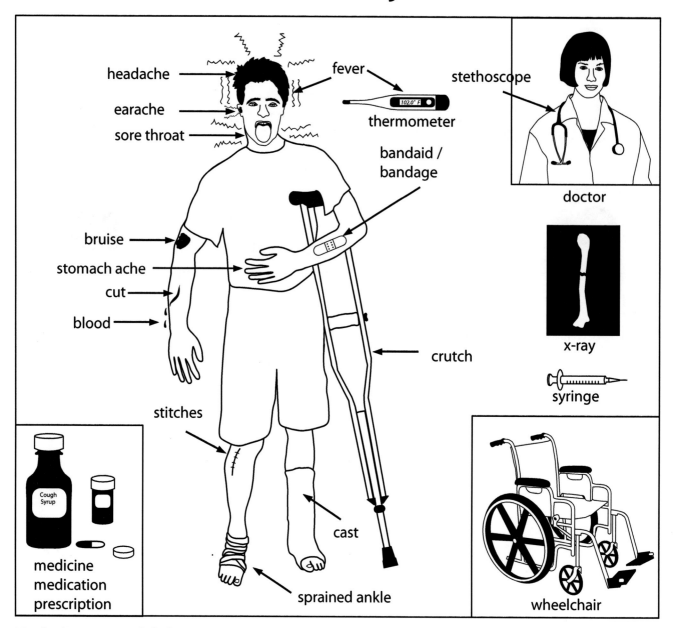

headache
earache
sore throat
fever
thermometer
stethoscope
doctor
bandaid / bandage
bruise
stomach ache
cut
blood
crutch
x-ray
syringe
stitches
cast
medicine
medication
prescription
sprained ankle
wheelchair

Underline *Yes, I did* if you ever had this illness or injury.
Underline *No, I didn't* if you did not.

1.	Did you ever have a sore throat?	Yes, I did.	No, I didn't.
2.	Did you ever have a sprained ankle?	Yes, I did.	No, I didn't.
3.	Did you ever have a fever?	Yes, I did.	No, I didn't.
4.	Did you ever have stitches?	Yes, I did.	No, I didn't.

Activity: Tell a partner about an illness or injury you had. Did you go to a doctor?

A to Z Picture Activities: Phonics and Vocabulary for Emerging Readers

Insects

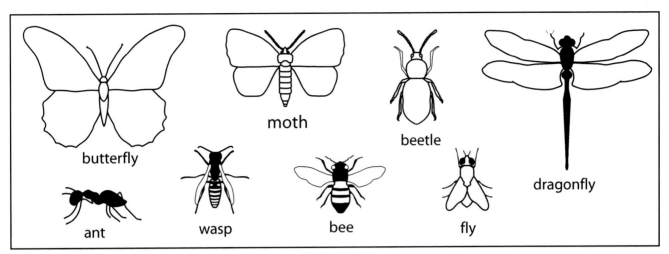

butterfly

moth

beetle

dragonfly

ant

wasp

bee

fly

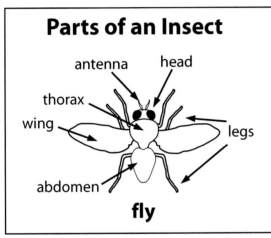

Parts of an Insect

antenna   head

thorax

wing

legs

abdomen

fly

1. This **fly** has _____ different parts.

2. It has _____6_____ legs, _____thorax,

   _____ wings, _____ abdomen,

   _____ head, _____ antennas/ae.

I

Write the name of an insect in the picture to complete the sentence. Ask a partner if you need help.

1. A_____*moth*_____ likes to fly near lights.

2. The wings of a_____ can have colors.

3. A_____ can make honey from flowers.

4. A_____ can sting you.

5. A_____ lives near the water.

Activity: Draw a picture of an insect and label its parts. You may draw any insect.

Jj Jump

jewelry

jet

jump

jam / jelly

jar

jeans

jigsaw puzzle

jacket

jog

Write a word from the picture to complete the sentence.

1. I have a _____ *jacket* _____ to wear on cold days.

2. A _____ is a very fast plane.

3. He likes to _____ into the swimming pool.

4. I like to eat _____ on bread.

Write your own sentence using words from the picture.

5. The _____ .

Jumping ?

Write *Yes, he (she) is* if the verb in the sentence matches the picture. Write *No, he (she) isn't* if the verb does not match.

1. Is he jumping? _____*Yes, he is.*_____
    (Yes, he is. / No, he isn't.)

2. Is she flying? _____
    (Yes, she is. / No, she isn't.)

3. Is he falling? _____
    (Yes, he is. / No, he isn't.)

4. Is she drinking? _____
    (Yes, she is. / No, she isn't.)

5. Is he driving? _____
    (Yes, he is. / No, he isn't.)

6. Is she eating? _____
    (Yes, she is. / No, she isn't.)

Activity: (1) Rewrite all the completed sentences above.

(2) Write six more questions of your own using different verbs.

Word Study: Joined Words

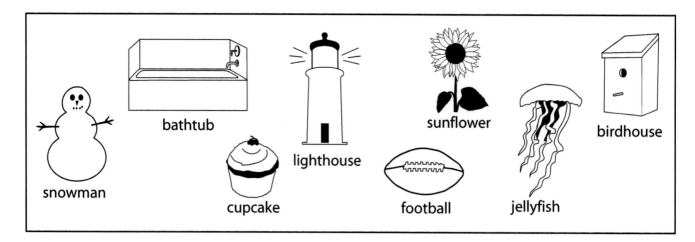

| snowman | bathtub | cupcake | lighthouse | sunflower | football | jellyfish | birdhouse |

Two or more words joined together make a compound word.

Write the **compound** word in the picture to complete each sentence.
Complete the sentence with the **compound** word for the picture.

1. A _____ *jellyfish* _____ body looks like jelly.

2. A _____ is a small cake.

3. I like to make a _____ when it snows.

4. A _____ is yellow like the sun.

5. The hole in the_____ is for the bird to enter.

6. There is a white_____ in the bathroom.

Jobs

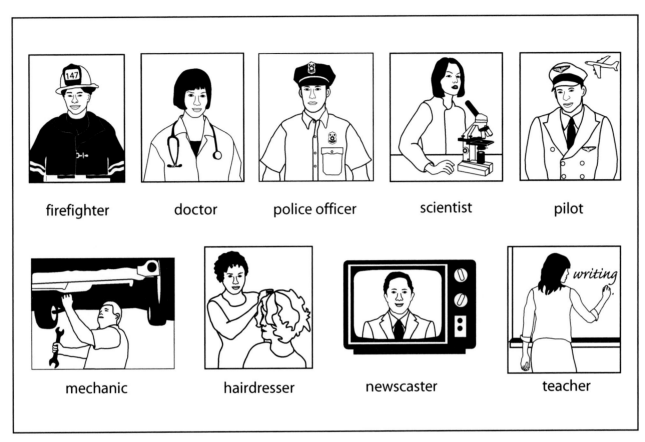

firefighter   doctor   police officer   scientist   pilot

mechanic   hairdresser   newscaster   teacher

Write the name of the job shown above to complete the sentence.

1. A person who fixes cars is a _____ *mechanic* _____.

2. A person who flies an airplane is a _____.

3. A person who helps students in a classroom is a _____.

4. A person who helps sick people is a _____.

5. A person who tells news on TV is a _____.

6. A person who helps put out fires is a _____.

Write about a job you would like. It can be any job. Tell why you would like this job.

7. I would like to be a _____ because

_____

_____.

K k kite

king

key

kite

kangaroo

kayak paddle

kayak

kitten

ketchup

kiss

kick

Between means *having something on each side.* Write a word from the picture to complete the sentence.

1. The key is betweeen the king and the _____ *kite* _____.

2. The kitten is between the kayak and the _____.

3. The kite is between the key and the _____.

4. The kayak is between the kayak paddle and the _____.

Write your own sentence using words from the picture.

5. The _____.

Kicking?

To make a question with the verb in the present progressive tense, we use this form:

kick - question form	
singular	*plural*
am I kicking? **are** you kicking? **is** he, **is** she, **is** it kicking?	**are** we kicking? **are** you kicking? **are** they kicking?

Use the chart above to complete the sentences.

1. Are they kissing? ____*Yes, they are.*____
(Yes, they are. / No, they are not.)

2. Are we kicking a ball? _____
(Yes, we are. / No, we are not.)

K

3. Are you eating? _____
(Yes, I am. / No, I am not.)

4. Are they flying? _____
(Yes, they are. / No, they are not.)

5. Are you cooking? _____
(Yes, we are. / No, we are not.)

6. Is she dancing? _____
(Yes, she is. / No, she is not.)

Activity: Use the chart to ask a partner questions with other verbs.

Phonics: Ck as K

ck

clock

lock

chicken

jacket   pocket

duck

sock

kick

The letters **ck** make the single **/K/** sound.

Complete the sentence with the **ck** word for the picture.

1. I have a _____ *lock* _____ on my bike.

2. The time on the _____ is 3:00.

3. The _____ has two pockets.

4. The _____ is by the sock.

5. He likes to _____ the soccer ball.

6. The _____ is in the water.

A to Z Picture Activities: Phonics and Vocabulary for Emerging Readers

Kitchen Items

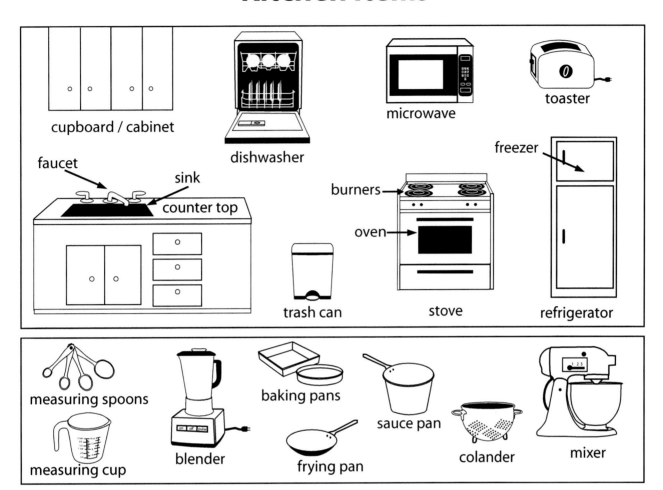

cupboard / cabinet

dishwasher

microwave

toaster

faucet

sink

counter top

burners

freezer

oven

trash can

stove

refrigerator

measuring spoons

baking pans

sauce pan

mixer

measuring cup

blender

frying pan

colander

K

1. Which of these items do you have in your kitchen? Write the words to complete the sentence.

     In my kitchen I have _____

_____

_____

_____

_____

_____

2. Tell a partner about your kitchen. Who cooks the food in your kitchen?

L l lion

light

leg

letter

lamp

lion

lip

line

lemon

listen

love

leaf

EXIT

laugh

lift

look at

leave

Write a word from the picture to complete the sentence.

1. She likes to _____*listen*_____ to music.

2. He is _____ a picture.

3. A lamp has a _____ inside it.

4. I _____ to be with my best friend.

Write your own sentence using words from the picture.

5. The _____ .

Let's listen!

Let's is the contraction for *let us*. *Let's* plus a verb is the way to suggest doing something. Write the verb on the line to suggest the action in the picture.

1. Let's _____*listen*_____ to this new song.

2. Let's _____ this new song.

3. Let's_____ the ball to the middle.

4. Let's _____ this bus.

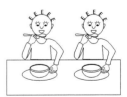

5. Let's_____ lunch now.

6. Let's_____ home by taxi.

Activity: Rewrite all the completed sentences above. Add five more suggestion sentences of your own using *Let's* plus different verbs. Look at pages 14, 22, 33, 40, and 56 for more verb ideas.

Phonics: Le, Al

le, al

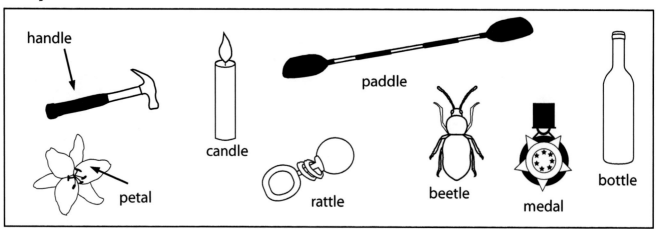

handle

candle

paddle

petal

rattle

beetle

medal

bottle

The letters **le** and **al** make the single **/L/** sound after the sounds **/T/** and **/D/**.
Complete the sentence with the **le** or **al** word for the picture.

1. A _____ *beetle* _____ is a kind of insect.

2. She used a _____ to make the kayak go.

3. The flower has a white _____ .

4. There is water in the _____ .

5. The hammer has a black _____ .

6. The _____ has a bright flame.

A to Z Picture Activities: Phonics and Vocabulary for Emerging Readers

Left and Right - Directions

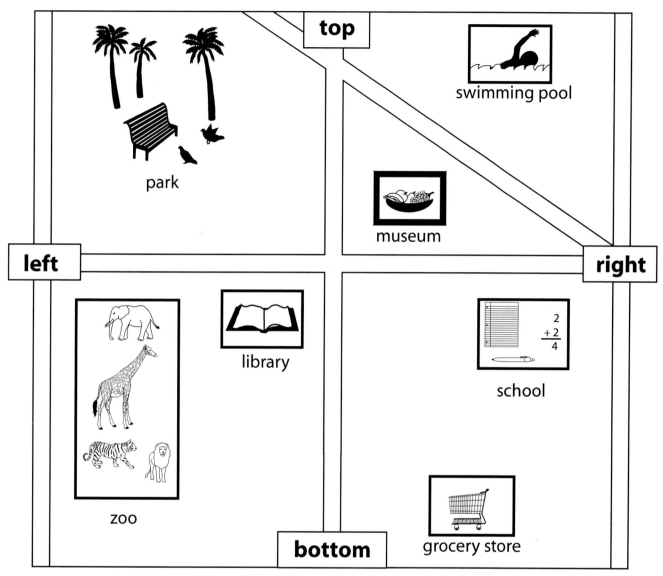

top

swimming pool

museum

left

right

park

library

school

zoo

bottom

grocery store

Complete the sentences, using locations on the map above. Use two of these phrases for each sentence: *on the left, on the right, at the top, at the bottom.*

1. The park is _____ *at the top, on the left* _____ .

2. The swimming pool is _____ .

3. The grocery store is _____ .

4. The zoo is _____ .

5. The school is _____ .

Activity: Make a map of your school or town. Tell a partner where things are.

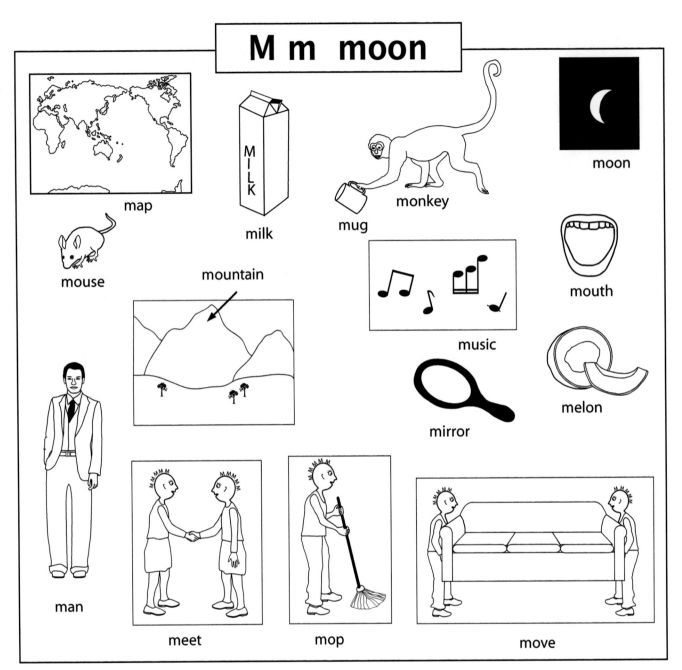

M m moon

map

milk

monkey

mug

moon

mouse

mountain

music

mouth

melon

mirror

man

meet

mop

move

Below means *under*. Write a word from the picture to complete the sentence.

1. The _____ *mouse* _____ is below the map.

2. The mirror is below the _____.

3. There is a melon below the _____.

4. The monkey is holding the _____.

Write your own sentence using words from the picture.

5. The _____.

May I...?

To ask permission of someone, you begin the question with *May I*. Write the verb that matches the picture to complete each question.

1. May I help you _____*move*_____ the sofa?

2. May I _____ your friend?

3. May I _____ the floor now?

4. May I _____ to that song?

5. May I _____ here, please?

6. May I _____ home with you?

Activity: Rewrite all the completed questions above. Write six more questions starting with *May I*.... Read the questions you wrote to a partner.

Phonics: Mb

mb

comb

thumb

climb

lamb

limb
(branch)

crumb

The letters **mb** at the end of a word make the **/M/** sound. The **b** is silent.

Complete the sentence with the **mb** word for the picture.

1. The tree has a long _____*limb*_____ at the bottom.

2. I like to_____ tall mountains.

3. The _____ is beside the mirror.

4. A _____ is a baby sheep.

5. I have four fingers and a _____ .

6. The mouse is eating the _____ .

M

Musical Instruments

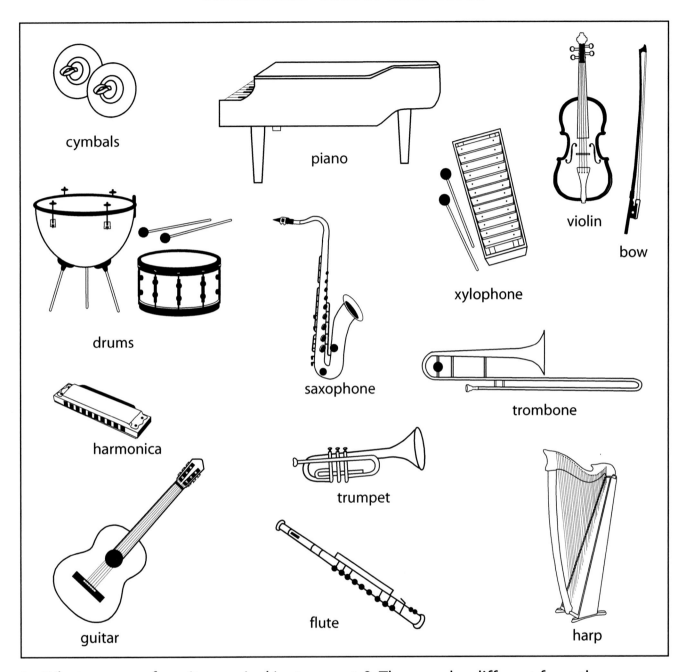

cymbals

piano

violin

bow

xylophone

drums

saxophone

trombone

harmonica

trumpet

flute

guitar

harp

1. What are your favorite musical instruments? They can be different from these.

    I like the _____

    _____

2. Ask a partner these questions:

    (a) Do you, or people in your family, play a musical instrument? Explain.

    (b) What is your favorite kind of music? Your favorite band? Why?

Meat and Dairy

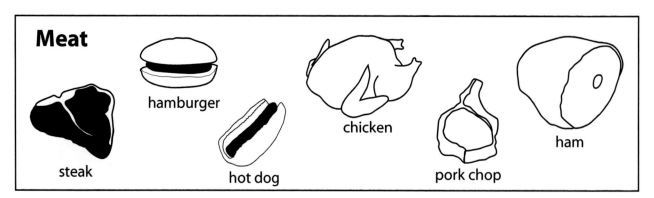

Do you eat meat and dairy foods? _____ yes _____ no

1. If you marked yes, list the meat and dairy foods that you eat.

    I eat: _____ *hamburger* _____   _____

    _____   _____

    _____   _____

    _____   _____

    _____   _____

2. Tell a partner about all your favorite foods.

    (a) Who shops for food in your family?

    (b) Who cooks the food?

Money and Math

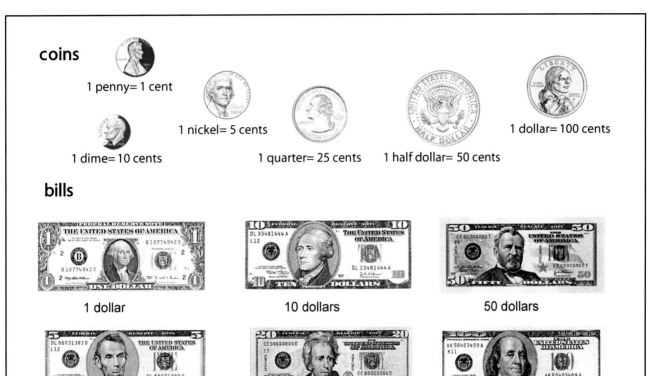

coins

1 penny= 1 cent

1 nickel= 5 cents

1 dime= 10 cents

1 quarter= 25 cents

1 half dollar= 50 cents

1 dollar= 100 cents

bills

1 dollar

10 dollars

50 dollars

5 dollars

20 dollars

100 dollars

Write the number to complete the addition sentence.

1. One quarter plus one nickel equals_____30_____cents.

2. Five dimes equals _____ cents.

3. Ten dollars plus ten dollars equals _____ dollars.

4. Twenty pennies equals_____dimes.

5. One half dollar equals_____quarters.

Activity: Ask a partner math questions using real coins and bills.

N n nest

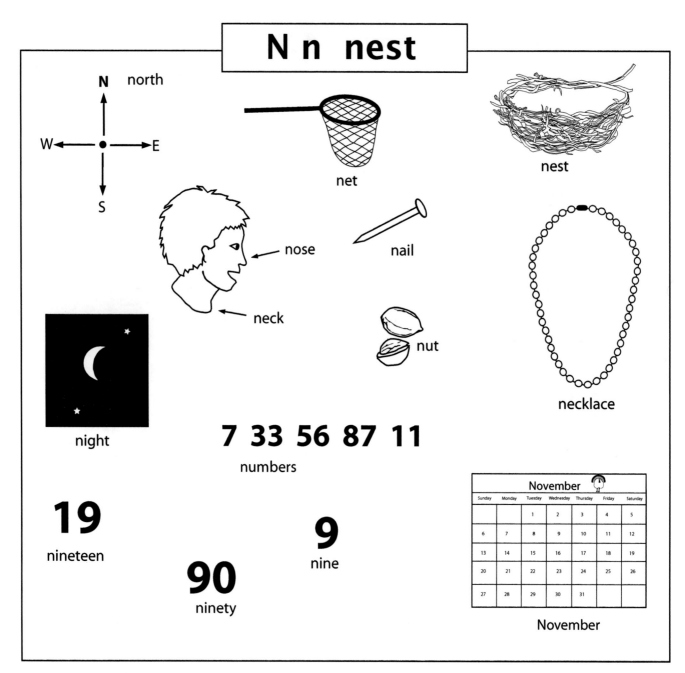

N north

W E

S

net

nest

nose

nail

neck

nut

necklace

night

7 33 56 87 11

numbers

19
nineteen

9
nine

90
ninety

				November 🍄			
Sunday	Monday	Tuesday	Wednesday	Thursday	Friday	Saturday
		1	2	3	4	5
6	7	8	9	10	11	12
13	14	15	16	17	18	19
20	21	22	23	24	25	26
27	28	29	30	31		

November

Write a word from the picture to complete the sentence.

1. The direction N on a compass arrow means _____ *north* _____.

2. He catches butterflies with a _____.

3. She is wearing a gold_____.

4. The moon and stars come out at _____.

Write your own sentence using words from the picture.

5. The _____.

No, Never!

Never means *not ever*. *Always* means *all the time*. *Sometimes* means *some of the time.*

Complete the sentence with *never, always,* or *sometimes* to match the picture.

1. A fish _____*never*_____ makes a nest in trees.
   (never, always, sometimes)

2. The sun _____ shines at night.
   (never, always, sometimes)

3. Music _____ makes you feel happy.
   (never, always, sometimes)

4. Plants _____ need water to grow.
   (never, always, sometimes)

5. Turtles _____ fly like birds.
   (never, always, sometimes)

6. The moon _____ shines at night.
   (never, always, sometimes)

Activity: Write six sentences about things you *always, sometimes,* or *never* do.
Read the sentences that you wrote to a partner.

Phonics: Kn and Gn

kn

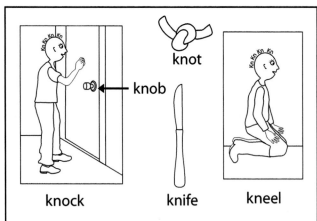

knot

knob

knock   knife   kneel

gn

design   sign   gnome

The letters **kn** or **gn** can also make the **/N/** sound. The **k** and **g** are silent. Complete the sentence with the **kn** or **gn** word for the picture.

1. The door has a round _____ _knob_ _____ on it.

2. A _____ is a little person, like an elf.

3. He cuts his meat with a _____ .

4. I always_____ before I enter the room.

5. There is a_____ in the rope.

6. Her skirt has a_____ .

A to Z Picture Activities: Phonics and Vocabulary for Emerging Readers

% Number Problems /Math Operations ✛

---

math operations

addition	subtraction	multiplication	division
6 + 6 = ☐12	12 − 6 = ☐6	2 x 6 = ☐12	12 ÷ 2 = ☐6
sum	*difference*	*product*	*quotient*

math symbols

+	**-**	**x**	**÷ or /**	**>**	**<**	**=**
plus	minus	times /multiplied by	divided by	greater than	less than	equal to

math terms

6	½ = 0.5 = 50%	1, 3, 5, 7, 9….	2, 4, 6, 8, 10… .
whole number	fraction decimal percent	odd numbers	even numbers

---

Write the number or word to complete the math sentence.

1. In the problem 2 + 2 = 4, the sum is the number _____4_____ .

2. In the problem 5 – 2 = 3, the difference is the number _____.

3. The decimal 0.5 is the same as ½ or _____ percent.

4. In the problem 5 x 5 = 25, the product is the number _____.

5. Three is an odd number, but four is an _____ number.

Activity: Write more math problems, and read them to a partner. Ask the partner to
write the problems you read.

O o octopus

order

office

octagon

octopus

orange

olives

on   off

1, 3, 5, 7, 9
odd numbers

ostrich

ox

1st, 2nd, 3rd, 4th
ordinal numbers

October

October

Sunday	Monday	Tuesday	Wednesday	Thursday	Friday	Saturday
		1	2	3	4	5
6	7	8	9	10	11	12
13	14	15	16	17	18	19
20	21	22	23	24	25	26
27	28	29	30	31		

Write a word from the picture to complete the sentence.

1. An _____*octopus*_____ is an animal with eight legs.

2. An _____ shape has eight sides.

3. Halloween is in the month of_____ .

4. The _____ has a desk and chair in it.

Write your own sentence using words from the picture.

5. The _____ .

A to Z Picture Activities: Phonics and Vocabulary for Emerging Readers

Opposites

Opposites are two things that are completely different, like *on* and *off.*

Look at the opposite words. Then complete the sentence to match the picture.

1. The light is _____*on*_____ .
    (on, off)

2. An ox is a _____ animal.
    (big, little)

3. The ostrich has _____ legs.
    (short, long)

4. Three and five are_____ numbers.
    (odd, even)

1, 3, 5, 7, 9

5. The kite is flying _____in the sky.
    (high, low)

6. The face looks_____ .
    (sad, happy)

Activity: Rewrite all the completed sentences above. Add two more sentences using other opposite words that you know. Read the sentences that you wrote to a partner.

Phonics: Short O and Or

o

frog

ox

sock

mop

or

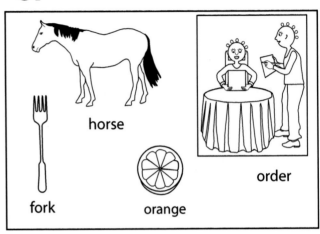

horse

fork

orange

order

Short o makes the sound **/uh/** as in *mop*. *Or* makes the sound in *fork*.

Complete the sentence with the *o* or *or* word for the picture.

1. A _____ *frog* _____ can hop and jump.

2. I have a _____ on my foot.

3. He eats salad with a _____ .

4. You can _____ dinner in a restaurant.

5. She likes to drink _____ juice.

6. An _____ has horns on its head.

A to Z Picture Activities: Phonics and Vocabulary for Emerging Readers

Phonics: Long O

o-e and o

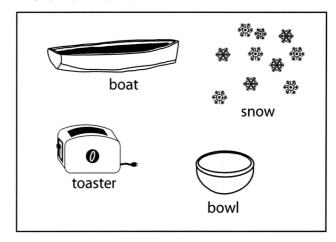

rope

colt

cold

bone

oa and ow

boat

snow

toaster

bowl

Long O: *o-e, o + some consonants, oa*, and **ow** make the sound **/O/**.

Complete the sentence with the **o, o-e, oa** or **ow** word for the picture.

1. Two olives are next to the _____*bowl*_____ .

2. I feel cold in the _____.

3. An octopus is by the _____.

4. The ox has a _____ on his neck.

5. A _____is a baby horse.

6. The x-ray shows a broken_____ .

Phonics: Ow and Ou

ow

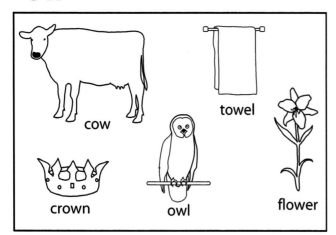

cow

towel

crown

owl

flower

ou

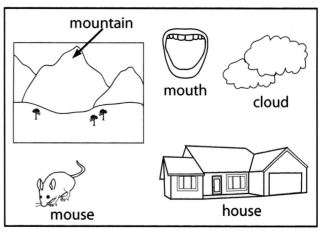

mountain

mouth

cloud

mouse

house

The letters **ow** or **ou** make the gliding sound **/OU/**, as in the words **now** and **out**.

Complete the sentence with the **ow** or **ou** word for the picture.

1. The king had a _____ *crown* _____ on his head.

2. There are clouds above the_____.

3. A cow is bigger than a _____.

4. An _____ is a bird that flies at night.

5. He opened his_____ for the dentist.

6. Flowers are growing by her _____.

A to Z Picture Activities: Phonics and Vocabulary for Emerging Readers

Phonics: Oy, Oi and Oo

oy

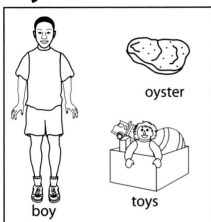

oyster

toys

boy

oi

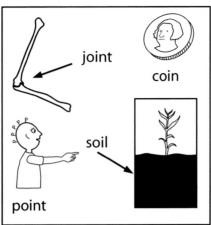

joint

coin

soil

point

oo

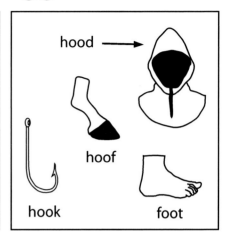

hood

hoof

hook   foot

The letters **oy** and **oi** make a gliding sound **/OY/**, as in the words **boy** and **coin**.
The letters **oo** can make the sound **/U/**, as in the word **book**.

Complete the sentence with the **oy**, **oi** or **oo** word for the picture.

1. An _____*oyster*_____ is a kind of shellfish.

2. A _____ is good in cold weather.

3. The little boy had a big box of _____ .

4. There is a _____ between the two bones.

5. The plant is growing in good _____ .

6. My _____ has five toes.

O

Ordinal Numbers

1st	first	13th	thirteenth	25th	twenty-fifth
2nd	second	14th	fourteenth	30th	thirtieth
3rd	third	15th	fifteenth	40th	fortieth
4th	fourth	16th	sixteenth	50th	fiftieth
5th	fifth	17th	seventeenth	60th	sixtieth
6th	sixth	18th	eighteenth	70th	seventieth
7th	seventh	19th	nineteenth	80th	eightieth
8th	eighth	20th	twentieth	90th	ninetieth
9th	ninth	21st	twenty-first	100th	one hundredth
10th	tenth	22nd	twenty-second	1000th	one thousandth
11th	eleventh	23rd	twenty-third	1,000,000th	one millionth
12th	twelfth	24th	twenty-fourth		

Ordinal numbers show the position in of something in a line or series.

example : The triangle is the <u>second</u> shape in the row.

Write the word for each ordinal number :

4th *fourth*   20th _____

11th _____   100th _____

5th _____   3rd _____

1st _____   8th _____

Activity: Ask a partner to write other ordinal numbers as you read them from the list.

Ovals, Octagons, and Other Shapes

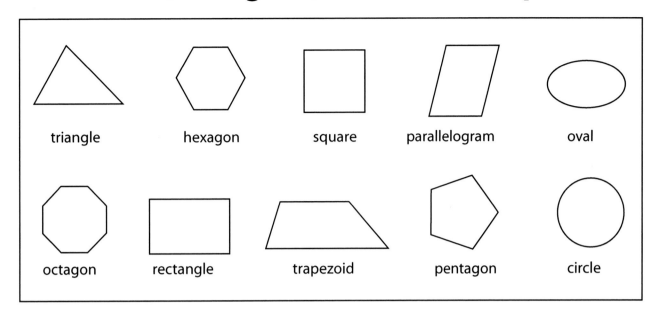

triangle   hexagon   square   parallelogram   oval

octagon   rectangle   trapezoid   pentagon   circle

Write the name of the shape from the picture to complete the sentence.

1. A round shape like the letter "o" is called a _____*circle*_____ .

2. A box shape with four equal sides is called a _____ .

3. A shape with eight sides is called an _____ .

4. A shape that looks like an egg is called an _____ .

5. A shape with five sides is called a _____ .

6. A shape with three sides is called a _____ .

7. A shape with six sides is called a _____ .

Activity: Draw a picture that has some of these shapes in it. Tell a partner about
your picture.

O

P p pear

paint

pan

pig

peanuts

pear

plant

piano

push

pants

pie

plate

peas

pull

pencil

pumpkin

paper

pizza

point

pen

Above means *over*. Write a word from the picture to complete the sentence.

1. The pig is above the _____ *piano* _____.

2. The pencil is above the_____.

3. The _____ is above the pie.

4. The peas are above the _____.

Write your own sentence using words from the picture.

5. The_____.

Pushed

To show that an action happened in the past, we add **ed** to the end of the regular verb.

push - *past tense*	
singular	*plural*
I push**ed** you push**ed** he, she, it push**ed**	we push**ed** you push**ed** they push**ed**

Write the verb that matches each picture to complete the sentence.

1. He _____*pushed*_____ the grocery cart.

         (pushed / painted)

2. She _____ the long rope.

       (watched / pulled)

3. You _____ right at me.

       (pushed / pointed)

4. I _____ a picture of a big pear.

     (painted / moved)

5. They _____ to music yesterday.

     (listened / lifted)

6. Last week we _____ the sofa.

     (kicked / moved)

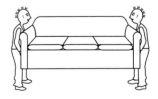

Activity: Write six sentences about what you did yesterday. Use regular verbs in the past tense. Read the sentences you wrote to a partner.

Word Study: Plurals

Plurals with **s**

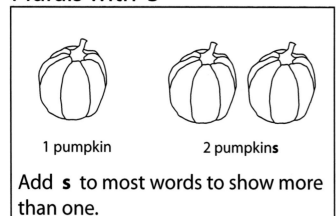

1 pumpkin   2 pumpkin**s**

Add **s** to most words to show more than one.

Plurals with **ies**

1 baby   2 bab**ies**

If a word ends in **y**, change **y** to **i** and add **es** to show more than one.

Plurals with **es**

2 bus**es**

2 dress**es**   2 brush**es**

2 church**es**   2 fox**es**

If a word ends in **s**, **ss**, **ch**, **sh**, or **x**, add **es** to show more than one.

Write the plural on the line beside the word.

1 inch, 2 _____*inches*_____

1 pan, 2 _____

1 penny, 2 _____

1 fox, 2 _____

1 dish, 2 _____

1 glass, 2 _____

A to Z Picture Activities: Phonics and Vocabulary for Emerging Readers

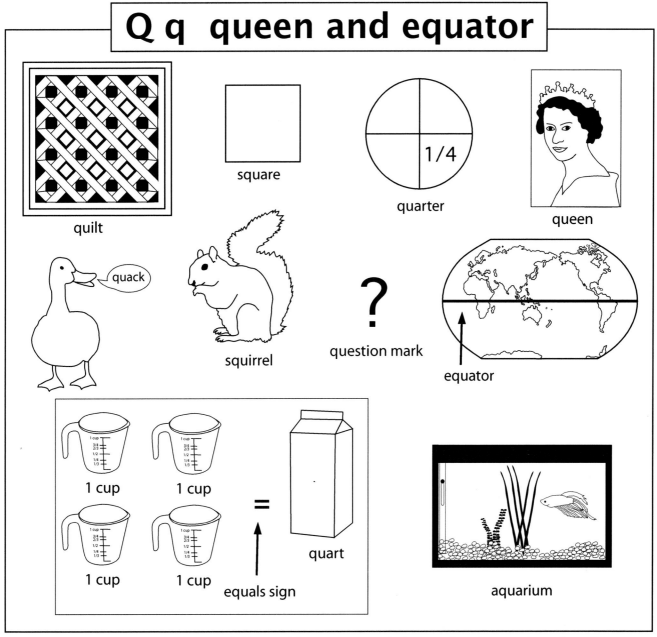

Q q queen and equator

quilt

square

1/4

quarter

queen

quack

squirrel

?

question mark

equator

1 cup

1 cup

1 cup

1 cup

=

quart

equals sign

aquarium

The letter **q** is almost always followed by **u** in English words. **Qu** makes the **/kw/** sound.

Write a **qu** word from the picture to complete the sentence.

1. One fourth of a circle is the same as a _____ *quarter* _____.

2. A _____ sometimes wears a crown.

3. The _____ has water, fish, and plants in it.

4. Four cups equal one _____.

5. The _____ is an imaginary line around the earth.

R r robot

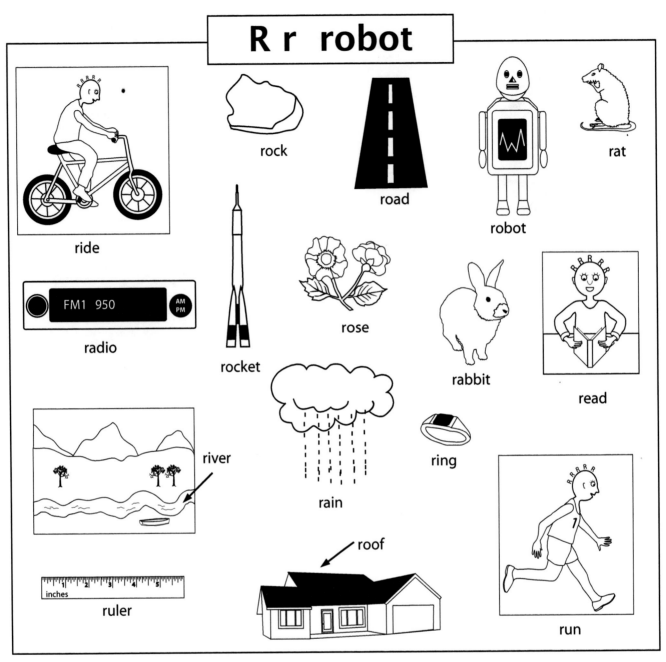

ride

rock

road

robot

rat

radio

rocket

rose

rabbit

read

river

rain

ring

ruler

roof

run

Write a word from the picture to complete the sentence.

1. He likes to _____*ride*_____ his bike on the road.

2. A _____ is a soft animal with big ears.

3. She listens to music on the _____ in her car.

4. To go to the moon, you must ride in a _____ .

Write your own sentence using words from the picture.

5. The _____ .

Did you run?

To form the negative past tense, we use *did not (or didn't)* plus the verb.

run - *past tense question form*	
singular	*plural*
Did I run?	**Did** we run?
Did you run?	**Did** you run?
Did he, she, it run?	**Did** they run?

Write the verb that matches each picture to complete the sentence.

1. Did they_____*run*_____ in that big race?
   (run / catch)

2. Did you_____ that new book?
   (ride / read)

3. Did I_____ you before?
   (meet / mop)

4. Did she _____ her bike?
   (ride / fly)

5. Did she _____the rice?
   (cook / paint)

6. Did he _____ there by taxi?
   (jump / go)

Activity: Ask a partner questions about last week. Start the questions with *Did you ...?*

R

Rulers and Measurements

We can use the English or the metric system to measure things.

Measures of length - How long?

1 inch = 2.54 centimeters

1 foot = 12 inches = 30.48 centimeters

1 yard = 36 inches = 3 feet = 0.91 meters

1 mile = 1,760 yards = 1.6 kilometers

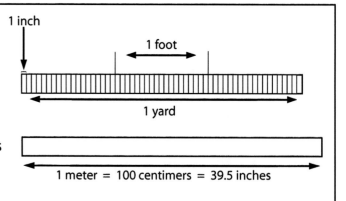

1 inch
1 foot
1 yard
1 meter = 100 centimers = 39.5 inches

Measures of weight - How heavy?

1 ounce = 28.35 grams

1 pound = 16 ounces = 453.6 grams

1 ton = 2000 pounds;   1 kilogram = 1000 grams

1 ounce | 28.35 grams

Measures of liquids - How much?

1 pint = 2 cups = 0.47 liters

1 quart = 2 pints = 0.95 liters

1 gallon = 4 quarts = 3.79 liters

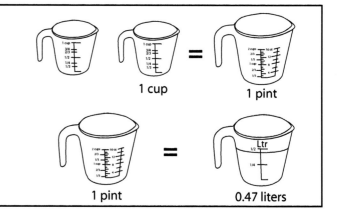

1 cup
1 pint
1 pint
0.47 liters

Use the charts above to complete these measurement sentences.

a. 2 yards equals____6____feet.   c. 2 pounds equals_____ounces.

b. 2 gallons equals_____ quarts.   d. 24 inches equals _____feet.

Activity: Find a ruler and measure the length of things around you. Make a chart
of the things and label each one in inches, feet, or centimeters.

Word Study: Comparatives and Superlatives

| 1 | 2 | 3 | | 1 | 2 | 3 |

Girl #2 has **longer** hair than girl #1.
Girl #3 has **the longest** hair.

Sock #2 is **smaller** than sock #1.
Sock #3 is **the smallest** sock.

We add **er** to the end of an adjective that compares two things and means **more**.

We add **est** to the end of an adjective that compares many things and means **most**.

Write the **er** ending (comparative) and **est** ending (superlative) for these adjectives.

	Comparative	Superlative
1. short	*short**er***	*short**est***
2. tall		
3. old		
4. new		
5. fast		
6. slow		
7. soft		
8. hard		

Activity: Ask a partner to make sentences with the words above. Use the sample
            sentences in the boxes as a model.

S s star

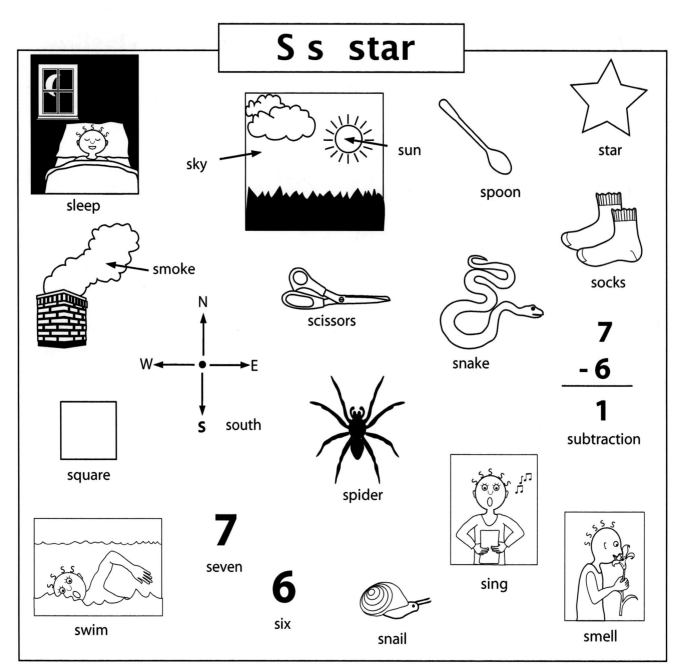

sleep

sky

sun

spoon

star

smoke

scissors

snake

socks

N
W — E
S   south

square

spider

$$\begin{array}{r} 7 \\ -\ 6 \\ \hline 1 \end{array}$$

subtraction

7
seven

6
six

swim

snail

sing

smell

Write a word from the picture to complete the sentence.

1. A _____ *square* _____ is a shape with four equal sides.

2. She likes to _____ her favorite songs.

3. The number that comes after six is _____ .

4. A _____ has eight legs.

Write your own sentence using words from the picture.

5. The _____ .

S

I did not swim.

To form the negative past tense, we use *did not* (or *didn't*) plus the verb.

swim - *past tense negative*	
singular	*plural*
I **did not** swim. You **did not** swim. He, she, it **did not** swim.	We **did not** swim. You **did not** swim. They **did not** swim.

Write the verb that matches each picture to complete the sentence.

1. I did not_____*swim*_____ because it was cold.
   (swim / stand)

2. She did not_____ well in the big bed.
   (sing / sleep)

3. We did not_____ him at school today.
   (swim / see)

4. He did not_____ on that chair.
   (sit / sleep)

5. They did not_____ the song with us.
   (sit / sing)

6. You did not_____ for the red light.
   (swim / stop)

Activity: When you tell someone about something you did not do, *did not* becomes *didn't*. Tell a partner what you *didn't* do today. Start with *I didn't ...* .

S

Word Study: Same-Sounding Words

Some words (homonyms) have the same sound but different meanings and spellings.

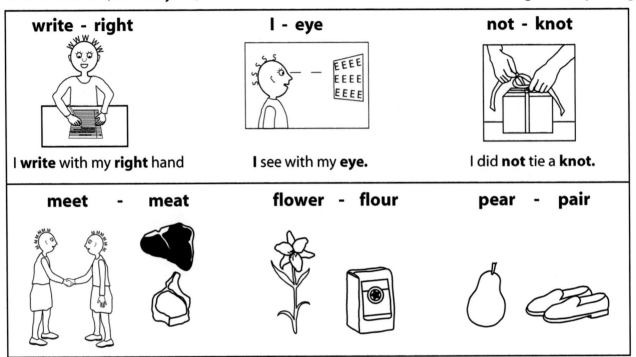

Write the word from the picture to complete the meaning of the sentence.

1. She has a pretty, red _____*flower*_____ in her garden.
   (flower, flour)

2. Turn _____ at the next street.
   (write, right)

3. He is wearing a new _____of tennis shoes.
   (pear, pair)

4. We were happy to _____ the new student.
   (meet, meat)

5. This is _____ the way to play the game.
   (not, knot)

6. Can you help me _____ this letter?
   (right, write)

Activity: Rewrite the sentences above with the words you chose.

Seasons and Weather

Seasons

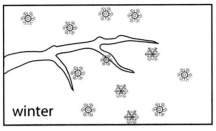
winter

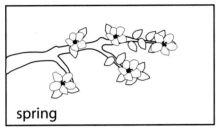
spring

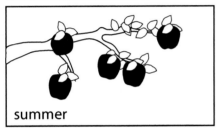
summer

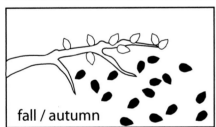
fall / autumn

Weather

sunny

cloudy

rainy

thunderstorm

snowy / cold

windy

Write the season or weather word from the picture to complete the sentence.

1. Weather can be snowy and cold in the _____ *winter* _____ .

2. Rainy days in the _____ help the new flowers grow.

3. It is fun to swim on the hot, sunny days of _____ .

4. Lightning can be a problem during a bad _____ .

5. Wind makes dry leaves fall in the _____ .

Activity: Were you ever in very bad weather? Tell a partner about it.

S

Sports

football
skiing
baseball
basketball
golf
soccer
tennis
track and field

Write the name of the sport from the picture to complete the sentence.

1. In _____*tennis*_____ , you hit a ball over the net.

2. In _____ , there are two goalies.

3. For_____ , you need snow.

4. In_____ , it helps to be very tall.

5. In _____ , you hit a ball with a bat.

6. In _____ , you wear pads and a helmet.

Activity: Tell a partner about your favorite sports. Are you on a team?

Seafood and Salad Items

Seafood

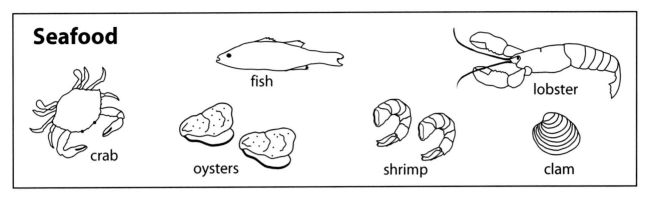

crab · fish · oysters · shrimp · lobster · clam

Salad

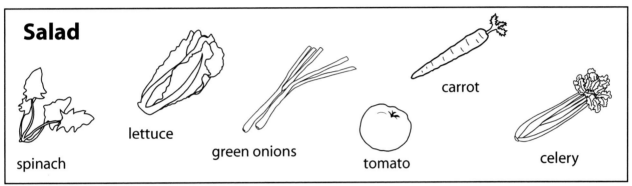

spinach · lettuce · green onions · carrot · tomato · celery

Do you eat salad? _____ yes _____ no   Do you eat seafood? _____ yes _____ no

1. If you marked yes, list the salad items and seafood that you eat.

   I eat: _____*tomatoes*_____   _____

   _____   _____

   _____   _____

   _____   _____

   _____   _____

2. Tell a partner about the kind of seafood and salad that you like.

   (a) What is your favorite fish? How do you like it cooked?

   (b) What is in your favorite salad?

S

T t tiger

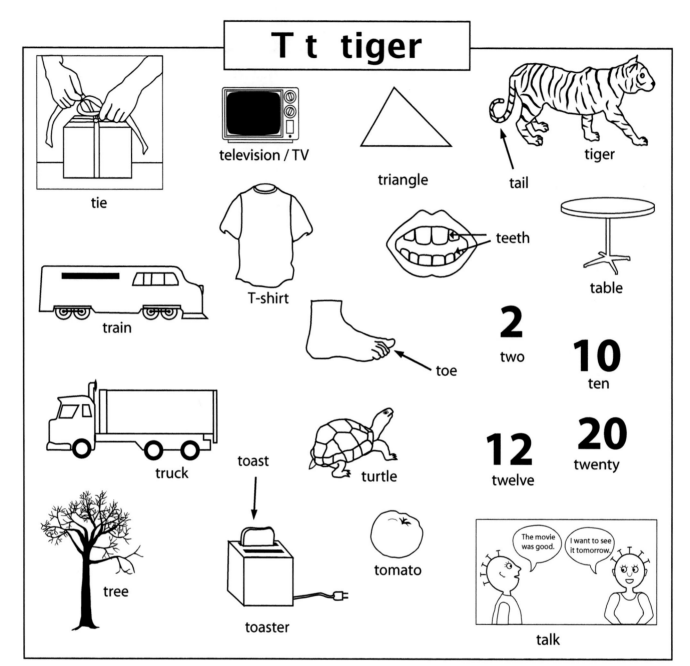

tie

television / TV

triangle

tail

tiger

T-shirt

teeth

table

train

toe

2 two

10 ten

truck

toast

turtle

12 twelve

20 twenty

tree

tomato

The movie was good.

I want to see it tomorrow.

toaster

talk

Write a word from the picture to complete the sentence.

1. She knows how to _____ *tie* _____ a bow on a gift.

2. A _____ is a big animal like a lion.

3. We like to watch football games on the _____.

4. A shape with three sides is called a _____.

Write your own sentence using words from the picture.

5. The _____.

 # True or False

Underline *true* if the statement is right. Underline *false* if the statement is wrong. Look at the pictures on the facing page to check the meanings of the words.

1. Two and tree are numbers.	True	<u>False</u>
2. A turtle has a long tail.	True	False
3. A toe is part of a foot.	True	False
4. A tomato is an animal.	True	False
5. A truck has white teeth.	True	False
6. A tiger can talk on the phone.	True	False
7. A train is bigger than a television.	True	False
8. A triangle has twelve sides.	True	False
9. Ten plus ten equals twenty.	True	False
10. A table can tie a knot.	True	False
11. A toaster can wear a T-shirt.	True	False
12. Twenty minus twelve equals eight.	True	False

Activity: On a separate paper:
      (a) Write all sentences that you marked *true*.
      (b) Rewrite the sentences that you marked *false* to make them *true*.
          For example, rewrite #1 as: Two and *three* are numbers.

Word Study: Two-Meaning Words

Some words have the same sound and spelling but different meanings.

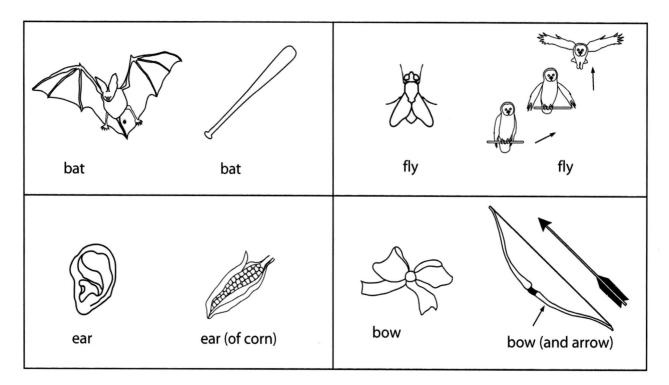

bat	bat	fly	fly
ear	ear (of corn)	bow	bow (and arrow)

Write the word that completes the meaning of the sentence.

1. He plays baseball with a wooden _____ *bat* _____.

2. I hear sounds with my _____ .

3. She loves to eat a hot _____ of corn with butter.

4. The bird hopped out of the nest and started to_____ .

5. The girl had a red _____ in her hair.

6. A _____ is an animal that comes out at night.

7. We don't want to see a black _____ on our food.

8. You can use a _____ and arrow to hunt animals.

Activity: Rewrite the sentences above with the words you chose.
Write other two-meaning words if you know some, like *tie* and *tie*.

A to Z Picture Activities: Phonics and Vocabulary for Emerging Readers

Transportation / Vehicles

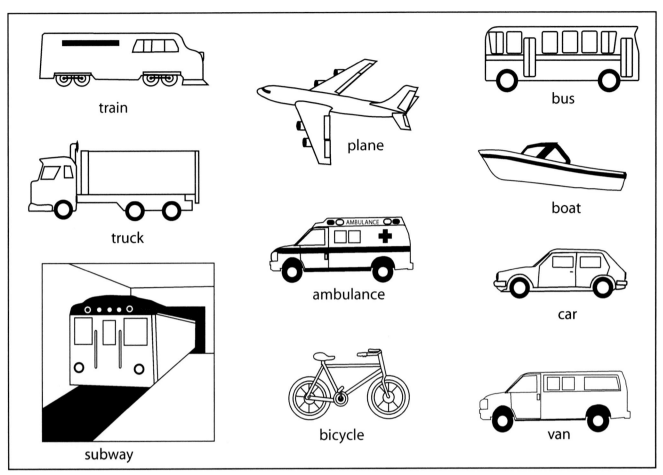

train

plane

bus

truck

boat

subway

ambulance

bicycle

car

van

Which kind of transportation? Write the name of the vehicle to complete the sentence.

1. Students often ride to school in a big yellow _____*bus*_____ .

2. The engine on a _____ can pull many freight cars.

3. He uses a _____ to go fishing in the ocean.

4. A _____ is an underground train in a city.

5. She can't find her_____ in the big parking lot.

6. The fastest way to travel is by _____ .

7. Boxes of food come to the grocery store by _____ .

8. To get to the hospital quickly, you need an _____ .

Activity: Rewrite the sentences above with the words you chose.

T

Telling Time

It is three o'clock.

It is one fifteen.
It is a quarter past one.

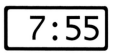

It is seven fifty-five.

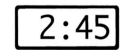

It is two forty-five.

It is twenty past ten.
It is ten twenty.

It is three thirty.
It is half past three.

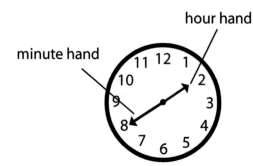

hour hand
minute hand

It is twenty minutes of two.
It is one forty.

What time is it? Read the times on the sample clocks above.
Write the words that match the time on each clock below.

1. It is _____*four-thirty*_____ .

2. It is _____ .

3. It is _____ .

9:20

4. It is _____ .

5. It is _____ .

11:35

A to Z Picture Activities: Phonics and Vocabulary for Emerging Readers

Tools

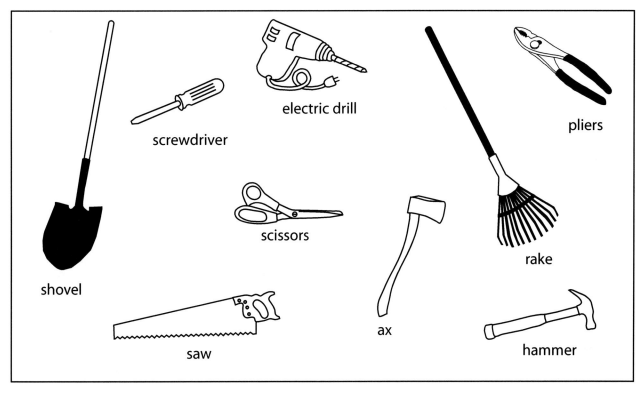

Which tool? Write the name of the tool from the picture to complete the sentence.

1. To dig a hole in the ground, you use a _____*shovel*_____.

2. You hit a nail into a wall with a _____ .

3. To cut a board, you use a _____.

4. You clean old leaves from the garden with a _____.

5. To cut paper or cloth, you use_____.

6. You use_____ to bend or twist wires.

Activity: Which tools do you have? Tell a partner how tools help you.

U u umpire

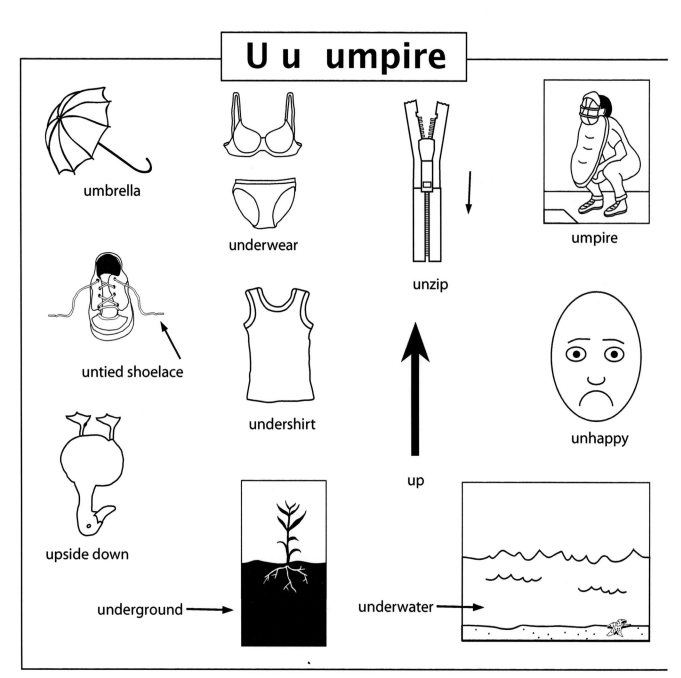

umbrella

underwear

unzip

umpire

untied shoelace

undershirt

unhappy

upside down

up

underground

underwater

Under means *below*. Write a word from the picture to complete the sentence.

1. There is an untied shoe under the _____ *umbrella* _____ .

2. The unhappy face is under the _____ .

3. The duck is turned_____ .

4. The black arrow points_____ .

Write your own sentence using words from the picture.

5. The _____ .

Un and Under

Un and *Under* can be added to the beginning of a word to change the meaning. *Un* means *not*, for example, so *unhappy* means *not* happy. *Under* means *below*, so *underwater* means *below* the water.

Write the word that matches the picture to complete the sentence.

1. He was wearing an _____ *undershirt* _____ .

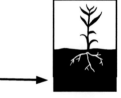

2. The jacket was hard to _____ .

3. The roots were growing _____ .

4. The tennis shoe is _____ .

5. She has a very_____ face.

6. A starfish lives_____ .

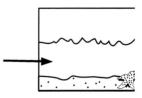

Activity: (a) Rewrite all the completed sentences above.

   (b) Find a dictionary, and look for more words that start with *un* and *under*. Write a list of words.

Phonics: Short U and Ur

u

umbrella

cup

sun

duck

ur

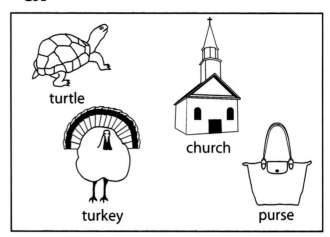

turtle

church

turkey

purse

Short u makes the sound **/UH/** as in *but*. *Ur* makes the sound **/ER/** as in *bird*.

Complete the sentence with the ***short u*** or ***ur*** word for the picture.

1. She uses an_____*umbrella*_____when it rains.

2. The _____ is a big Thanksgiving bird.

3. She had a _____of coffee for breakfast.

4. In summer, the_____ is often hot.

5. A_____ can pull its head into its shell.

6. The woman put her money in a_____.

    A to Z Picture Activities: Phonics and Vocabulary for Emerging Readers

Phonics: Long U

u-e, ue, ui, oo, and ew

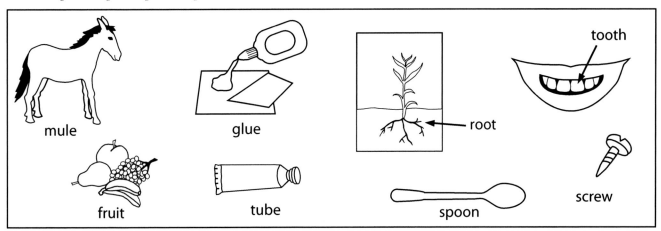

mule
glue
root
tooth
fruit
tube
spoon
screw

U-e, ue, ui, oo, or *ew* words make the sound /OO/ in the word *school*.

Complete the sentence with the *u-e, ue, ui, oo,* or *ew* word for the picture.

1. She used _____*glue*_____ to make a valentine.

2. Bananas are a kind of _____.

3. We usually eat ice cream with a _____.

4. Toothpaste comes in a _____.

5. The plant has a deep, long _____.

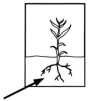

U

6. He turned the _____ with a screwdriver.

V v van

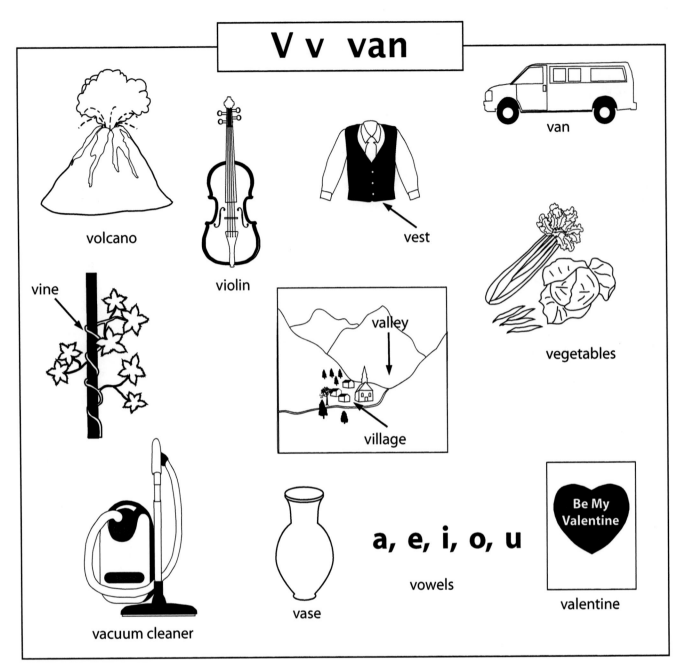

volcano

violin

vest

van

vine

valley

village

vegetables

vacuum cleaner

vase

a, e, i, o, u

vowels

Be My Valentine

valentine

Write a word from the picture to complete the sentence.

1. Hot lava flowed out of the _____ *volcano* _____.

2. We like to make soup with lots of _____.

3. He played sweet music on the _____.

4. She put flowers and water in the _____.

Write your own sentence using words from the picture.

5. The _____.

A to Z Picture Activities: Phonics and Vocabulary for Emerging Readers

V

Verb Review

walking, talking, listening, kissing, reading, sleeping, swimming, pointing

Write the verb from the list that matches the picture in each sentence.

1. He is_____*pointing*_____at us.

2. She is_____.

3. They are_____.

4. I am_____.

5. We are _____.

6. Are you_____?

7. Is she_____?

8. Are they_____?

V

Verb Review

pulling, laughing, painting, holding, smelling, riding, sitting, mopping

Write the verb from the list that matches the picture near each sentence.

1. He was _____*pulling*_____ the rope.

2. She was_____ the hen.

3. I was_____ there.

4. Were you_____the pear?

5. Was he_____ his bike?

6. Were they_____at us?

7. I was_____that flower.

8. He was_____ the floor.

A to Z Picture Activities: Phonics and Vocabulary for Emerging Readers

Vegetables

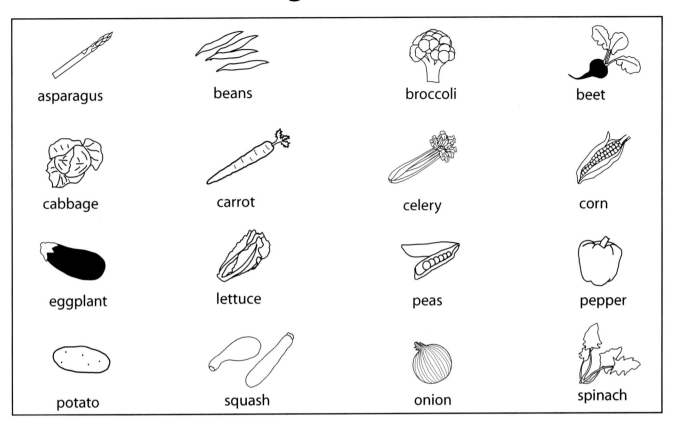

asparagus   beans   broccoli   beet

cabbage   carrot   celery   corn

eggplant   lettuce   peas   pepper

potato   squash   onion   spinach

Vegetables and Colors

Put an X by the color (or colors) of these vegetables. If you are not sure, look at the color chart on the back cover.

Vegetables	red / purple	green	yellow	orange	white
beet	x				
broccoli					
carrot					
corn					
lettuce					
onion					
pepper					
potato					
squash					

V

W w watch

web

west

wing

wasp

watch

walk

woman

window

wake up

wolf

write

wash

water

wall

wait

wave

Write a word from the picture to complete the sentence.

1. I _____ *wake up* _____ every morning at seven o'clock.

2. He had to_____a long time for his plane.

3. I opened the _____ and watched the snow.

4. A _____is an animal that looks like a dog.

Write your own sentence using words from the picture.

5. The _____ .

We will walk.

To show that an action is going to happen in the future, we put *will* before the verb.

walk - *future tense*	
singular	*plural*
I **will** walk	we **will** walk
you **will** walk	you **will** walk
he, she, it **will** walk	they **will** walk

Write the verb that matches each picture to complete the sentence in the future tense.

1. We _____ *will walk* _____ to the store with you.
   (will wash / will walk)

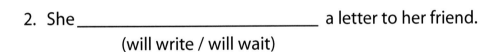

2. She _____ a letter to her friend.
   (will write / will wait)

3. I _____ at 7:30 tomorrow.
   (will walk / will wake up)

4. He _____ the clothes later.
   (will wait / will wash)

5. They _____ TV with us tonight.
   (will watch / will wash)

6. You _____ at the airport.
   (will wake up / will wait)

W

Activity: Tell a partner what you *will* do tomorrow. Use verbs in the future tense.

Word Study: Words as Parts of Speech

Words can be classified by their use as *parts of speech* in a sentence.
Example sentence: **The woman walked slowly to the open window.**
The part of speech for each word in the sentence is shown below with a ★.

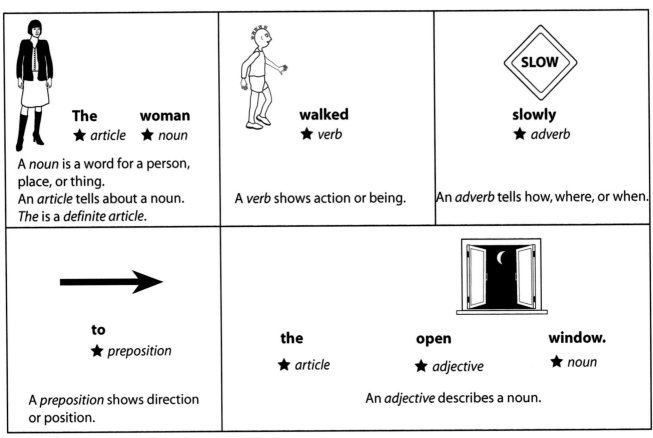

The **woman** ★ *article* ★ *noun* A *noun* is a word for a person, place, or thing. An *article* tells about a noun. *The* is a *definite article*.	**walked** ★ *verb* A *verb* shows action or being.	**slowly** ★ *adverb* An *adverb* tells how, where, or when.
to ★ *preposition* A *preposition* shows direction or position.	**the** **open** **window.** ★ *article* ★ *adjective* ★ *noun* An *adjective* describes a noun.	

Write the part of speech from the picture to complete the sentence

1. The word **woman** is a _____ *noun* _____.

2. The word **walked** is a _____.

3. The word **open** is an _____.

4. The word **slowly** is an _____.

5. The word **window** is a _____.

6. The word **to** is a _____.

7. The word **the** is an _____.

W

Who, What, Where, When, and Why?

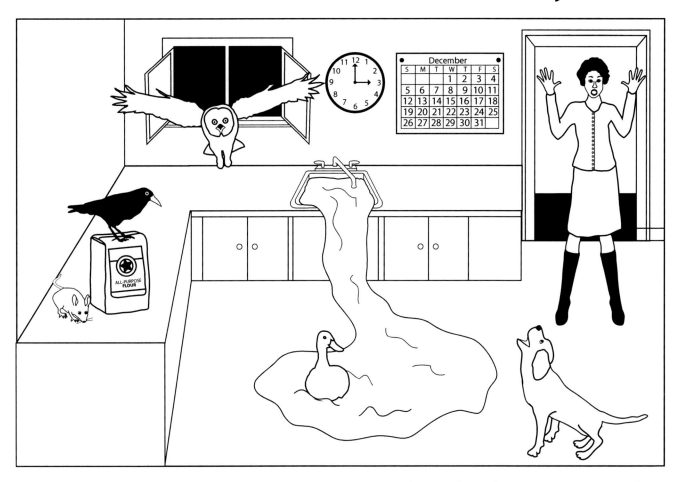

Who, what, where, when, and *why* are question words. Look at the picture to complete the answers to the questions.

1. **What is wrong in this picture?** There is an owl in the _____*kitchen*_____.

2. **Who is surprised?** The _____ is surprised.

3. **Where is the duck?** The duck is swimming in the _____.

4. **When did the woman enter the kitchen?** She entered at _____.

5. **Where is the crow?** The crow is on the _____.

6. **What month of the year is it?** It is _____.

7. **Why is the dog howling?** The dog is howling because _____

_____

Activity: Ask a partner more questions that start with *who, what, where, when,* or *why.*

W

X x exit

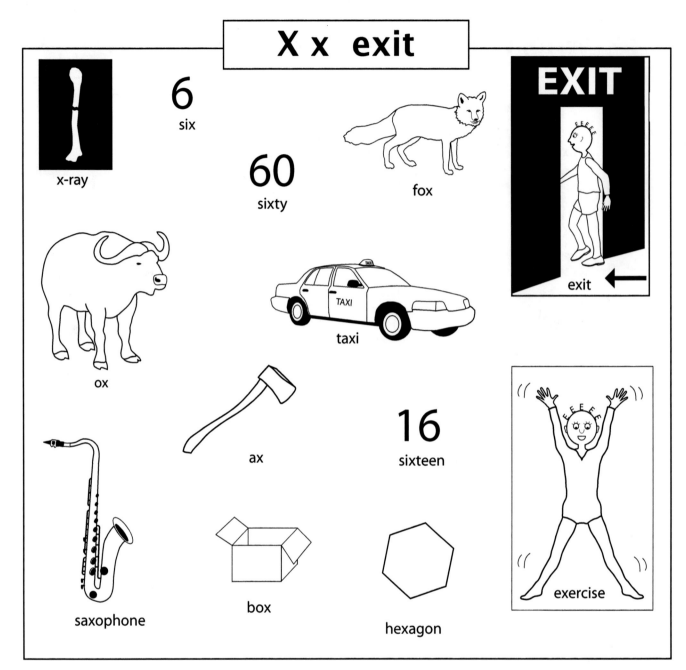

x-ray

6 six

60 sixty

fox

EXIT
exit

ox

taxi

ax

16 sixteen

saxophone

box

hexagon

exercise

Write a word from the picture to complete the sentence.

1. There is an _____*x-ray*_____ of his broken bone.

2. They opened the _____ of holiday candy.

3. Running is good _____ .

4. A _____ is a shape with six sides.

Write your own sentence using words from the picture.

5. The _____ .

X

A to Z Picture Activities: Phonics and Vocabulary for Emerging Readers

Extra Questions: Will you...?

To ask a question in the future tense, we begin the question with *will*.

future tense - question form	
singular	*plural*
Will I exercise?	**Will** we exercise?
Will you exercise?	**Will** you exercise?
Will he, she, it exercise?	**Will** they exercise?

Write the verb that matches each picture to complete the sentence in the future tense.

1. ___*Will you exercise*_____ today at school?
   (Will you exercise / Will you exit)

2. _____ there by taxi?
   (Will he go / Will he write)

3. _____ at 7:00?
   (Will we wake up / Will we exit)

4. _____ for me?
   (Will she wait / Will she exercise)

5. _____ that book?
   (Will you run / Will you read)

6. _____ their clothes?
   (Will they wash / Will they wake up)

Activity: Ask a partner what he or she *will* do tomorrow. Begin the question *Will you.*

X

Y y yarn

yolk

yogurt

yarn

yo-yo

yoga

yell

yam

yard

yak

yawn

Write a word from the picture to complete the sentence.

1. They liked to do_____ *yoga* _____for exercise.

2. Inside the egg, there was a yellow_____ .

3. He was very sleepy and started to_____ .

4. A _____is a vegetable like a potato.

Write your own sentence using words from the picture.

5. The _____ .

If a yoyo....

We use *if* when something might happen, but we are not sure.
Underline *yes* if the statement is true. Underline *no* if the statement is not true.

Look at the pictures on the facing page to check the meanings of the words.

1. If a yoyo is working, it goes up and down. <u>Yes</u>　　　　No

2. If an egg falls, the yoga will spill out. 　　Yes　　　　No

3. If I yawn, I am probably sleepy. 　　Yes　　　　No

4. If a yak eats a yam, it will say, "yummy." 　　Yes　　　　No

5. If you have a yard, you can grow yogurt. 　　Yes　　　　No

6. If you cook a yam, it gets soft. 　　Yes　　　　No

7. If you yell at an egg yolk, it will dance. 　　Yes　　　　No

8. If you have a ball of yarn, you can fly. 　　Yes　　　　No

9. If you yell in class, students will sleep. 　　Yes　　　　No

10. If you are yawning, your mouth is closed. 　　Yes　　　　No

11. If you like to exercise, you might like yoga. 　　Yes　　　　No

12. If you are yelling, your mouth is open. 　　Yes　　　　No

Activity: Tell a partner why you answered *yes* or *no*. Did the partner have the same answers? Write some sentences of your own that start with *If....*

Y

Phonics: Y as a Vowel

y as /AY/

frying pan

sky

cry

y as /EE/

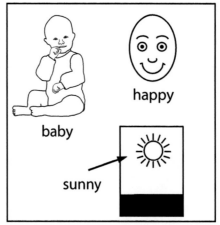

happy

baby

sunny

y as /I/

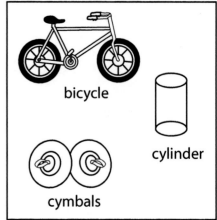

bicycle

cylinder

cymbals

The letter **y** at the middle or end of a word is considered a vowel.
It can make three sounds: (1) the **/AY/** sound in **sky**; (2) the **/EE/** sound in **baby;** or
(3) the **/I/** sound in **cymbals**.

Complete the sentence with the **y - vowel** word for the picture.

1. She was sad and started to _____ *cry* _____ .

2. A _____ has two wheels.

3. He was a very happy_____ .

4. There is blue_____ on a sunny day.

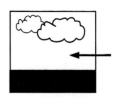

5. I cooked an egg in the _____ .

6. There is the sound of _____ in the music.

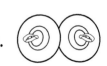

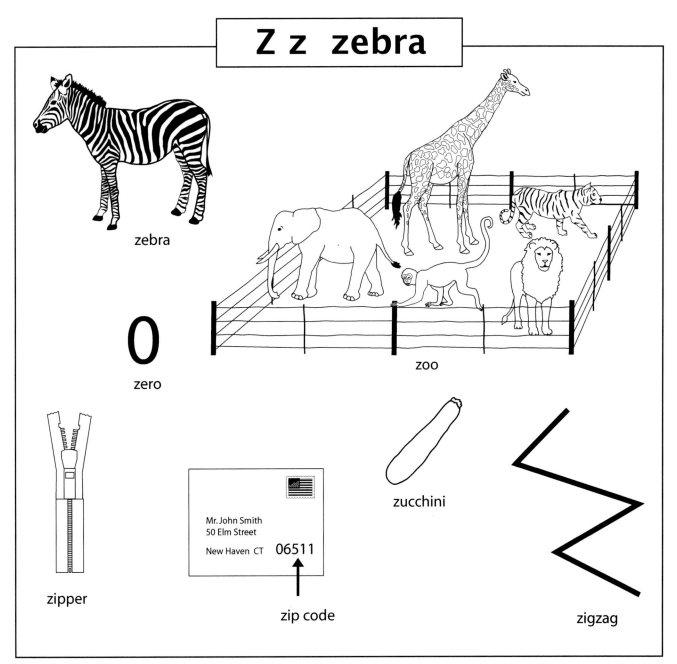

Z z zebra

zebra

zero

zoo

zipper

zip code

zucchini

zigzag

Write a word from the picture to complete the sentence.

1. Her zip code has a _____ *zero* _____ in it.

2. To close the jacket, you pull up on the _____ .

3. There are many wild animals in a _____ .

4. A _____ is a kind of squash.

Write your own sentence using words from the picture.

5. The _____ .

Pizza and Pretzels

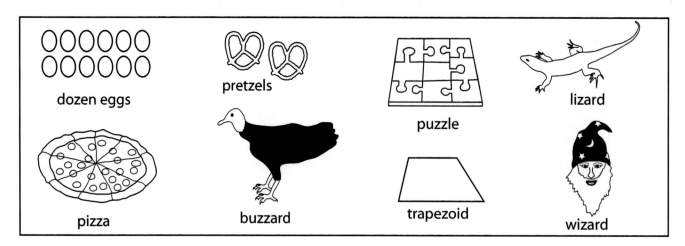

dozen eggs

pretzels

puzzle

lizard

pizza

buzzard

trapezoid

wizard

Some words have **z** in the middle. Others begin with **z**, as on the facing page.

Write complete sentences using as many z-words as you can. Use the example as a model.

example: *I like to eat pizza and pretzels at the zoo.*

1. _____

_____

2. _____

_____

3. _____

_____

4. _____

_____

To the Teacher

What is an Emerging Reader? The *PreK-12 English Language Proficiency Standards* (TESOL, 2006) specifies the term "emerging" to describe level 2 English language learners as follows:

> *At the Emerging level, students can understand phrases and short sentences....*
> *Reading and writing proficiency may vary depending upon students' literacy development in their native language and their familiarity with the alphabet, among other factors. Students can read words and phrases and locate specific, predictable information in simple, everyday, or environmental print. They often make errors in writing that hinder communication.*

Level 2 emerging learners, therefore, are often older students who can already read in their first language but need contrastive phonics and intensive vocabulary to develop English literacy.

What is the purpose of this book? *A to Z Picture Activities* is an illustrated English vocabulary builder with phonics and grammar exercises for emerging readers from grade 6 to adult. All of its 888 illustrated words are presented in the context of lively art and sentence activities. Each unit includes oral practice as well as introductory reading and writing.

How can the book be used? The book can be used as a sequenced program from A to Z or selectively as a supplement to another text. To ensure the most systematic and comprehensive approach to the sounds and spellings of English, however, it is recommended that teachers proceed from A to Z, since most exercises are designed cumulatively. The vocabulary activity pages include 150 of the most frequent words in English, the Dolch List of basic sight words, 62 illustrated common verbs, and 550 words on themes such as colors, clothing, and food. These pages can be used at any time.

How do I present A to Z Picture Activities to my students?

- First orient your students to the components of the book, including the pages at the end – the "CD Script for the A to Z Activities Book," the "Activities Answer Key," and the "Index of Illustrated Words."

- Help the students fill in page iii, "All About Me" to personalize the book. This page also provides you information about each student. Then discuss page vi, "The Sounds of English."

- Go over page 1, "The Alphabet," with your students. Here you can explain that the names of the alphabet letters in English frequently do not correspond with the sounds they represent. On the phonics pages they will learn more about sound-symbol correspondence and spelling.

- Read the title of the first page of the A unit to the students. Ask them to skim all the A unit pages. Explain that there are vocabulary, grammar, and phonics exercises in each unit.

- Pronounce the illustrated vocabulary for the students. Discuss the meanings of the words, and play the CD of the page, having the students repeat the words. Alternatively, you can read the CD script for the first page from the printout in the back of the book.

- Read the activity instructions aloud. Ask a student to read and explain the example sentence. Divide the students into pairs. Have them complete the page and discuss their answers. Remind them that they can check their answers in the back of the book.

- Continue similarly with the phonics pages and vocabulary pages. Follow this same process for each unit. Discuss and review the vocabulary, phonics, and key grammar points in the unit.

CD Script for *The A to Z Activity Book*

Track 1, pages 2, 4, 5, and 6.

Page 2. The letter A can be pronounced in many different ways.
   Say these words: address alphabet alligator ax apple acrobat airplane ant ambulance ask addition arm arrow

Page 4. The letter A can be the short A sound pronounced /A/ as in /HAT/.
   Say these words: hat man apple map

   The letter A followed by the letter R is pronounced /AH/ as in /AHRM/.
   Say these words: arm car star jar

Page 5. The letters AI, AY, and A with the letter E at the end of the word are the long A sound pronounced /AI/ as in /TAIP/.
   Say these words: cake tape plate rain paint tail tray May day

Page 6. The letter A followed by the letters L, W, and U makes the sound /AW/ as in /BAWL/.
   Say these words: ball fall chalk salt walk saw saucer claw draw August

Track 2, pages 10 and 12.

Page 10. The letter B is pronounced /BUH/ as in /BUHS/.
   Say these words: bear bug bird ball branch bag bike bus butterfly box brush bread bowl banana book boy bed

Page 12. The two-letter blend BL is pronounced /BLUH/ as in /BLAHKS/.
   Say these words: blocks black blanket blouse

   The two-letter blend BR is pronounced /BRUH/ as in /BRANCH/.
   Say these words: branch brush bread broom

Track 3, pages 14 and 16.

Page 14. The letter C can be pronounced /KUH/ before many vowel sounds as in /KOU/ and before consonants as in /KLOUD/.
   Say these words: cow cap cloud catch cut cook cup cat crayon coat crown car carrot clock cake

Page 16. The letter C can also be pronounced /SUH/ before the vowel sounds /E/, /ER/, and /I/ as in /SENTER/, /SERKuhL/, and /SITEE/.
   Say these words: celery circle center face bicycle

   The letters CH are pronounced /CHUH/ as in /CHIN/.
   Say these words: chair chin chicken cheese

A to Z Picture Activities: Phonics and Vocabulary for Emerging Readers

Track 4, pages 22 and 24.

Page 22. The letter D can be pronounced /DUH/ as in /DESK/.
Say these words: desk drawer dolphin drive draw drink dance diamond door down dog drum doll dress dollar duck

Page 24. *Say these ending blends:* drink desk diamond belt jump list gift milk

Track 5, pages 26, 28, and 29.

Page 26. The letter E can be pronounced as the short E , /E/ as in /EL/.
Say these words: elevator eleven elephant exit enter envelope egg engine elbow exercise

Page 28. The letter E can be pronounced as the short E , /E/ as in /BEL/.
Say these words: bell hen egg pen

The letters ER can be pronounced /ER/ as in /HER/.
Say these words: paper water fern ruler

Page 29. The letters EA and EE are often pronounced /EE/ as in /SEE/.
Say these words: eagle eat hear ear tree see teeth sheep

Track 6, pages 32 and 34.

Page 32. The letter F can be pronounced /FUH/ as in /FUHN/.
Say these words: foot fin fish fly fruit frog floor fall fifteen flag fork fire flame flute five

Page 34. The letters PH and GH are pronounced like the sound /FUH/.
Say these words: phone elephant alphabet cough laugh

Track 7, pages 40 and 42.

Page 40. The letter G can be pronounced as the hard G sound /GUH/ as in /GO/.
Say these words: glass gorilla grass go grapes goat grow gift game give get off get on glasses girl gate garden glove gum gas

Page 42. The soft G sound is often followed by the letters I or silent E, as in /PAIJ/.
Say these words: giraffe giant cabbage page

The letters NG are pronounced /NG/ as in /SING/.
Say these words: hanger song sing ring

Track 8, pages 44 and 46.

Page 44. The letter H is pronounced /HUH/ as in /HEN/.
Say these words: hear hole hen hot dog horse hundred hold hair head handle hammer house hop hill hit hug hand hat

Page 46. Digraphs are two letters that together make a single sound. SH makes the sound /SH/ as in /FISH/. TH can make the sound /th/ as in /BOth/, or the sound /TH/ as in /THUH/. WH can make the sound /HW/ as in /HWAIL/.
Say these words: shirt shoe shark moth three thumb wheel whistle whale

Track 9, pages 50, 52, and 53.

Page 50. The letter I often makes the short / I/ sound as in /INGK/.
Say these words: inch igloo insect injury ink iguana index finger invitation it's invited ill

Page 52. The letter I often makes the short /I/ sound as in /FISH/.
Say these words: inch sit kiss fish

The letters IR make the sound /ER/ as in /BERD/.
Say these words: girl shirt bird skirt

Page 53. The long I sound /AY/ can be made with silent E, Y, and IGH.
Say these words: ice drive bike fly fry frying pan sky light thigh night

Track 10, page 56.

Page 56. The letter J makes the sound /JUH/ as in /JAM/.
Say these words: jewelry jet jump jar jam jelly jog jacket jigsaw jeans

Track 11, pages 60 and 62.

Page 60. The letter K makes the sound /KUH/ as in /KEE/.
Say these words: king key kite kangaroo kitten ketchup kick kiss kayak kayak paddle

Page 62. The letters CK make the /KUH/ sound as in /DUHK/.
Say these words: clock lock chicken jacket pocket duck sock kick

Track 12, pages 64 and 66.

Page 64. The letter L makes the sound /LUH/ as in /LEG/.
Say these words: light leg letter lip lamp lion lemon line leaf leave look at lift love laugh listen

Page 66. The letters LE and AL after a /D/ or /T/ sound make the sound /LLL/ as in /BAHTL/.
Say these words: handle candle paddle bottle medal beetle rattle petal

Track 13, pages 68 and 70.

Page 68. The letter M makes the sound /MMM/ as in /MAP/.
Say these words: mouse map milk mug monkey moon mouth music mirror mountain melon move mop meet man

Page 70. The letters MB at the end of a word make the /MMM/ sound. The letter B has no sound.
Say these words: comb thumb climb lamb crumb limb

Track 14, pages 74 and 76.

Page 74. The letter N makes the sound /NNN/ as in /NET/.
Say these words: north net nest nail nose neck nut necklace November nine numbers ninety nineteen night

Page 76. The letters KN and GN can make the sound /NNN/ as in /NAYF/.
Say these words: knock knob knife knot kneel design sign gnome

Track 15, pages 78, 80, 81, 82, and 83.

Page 78. The letter O can make many different sounds.
Say these O words: order office octagon octopus off on olives odd numbers October ox ordinal numbers ostrich orange

Page 80. The letter O can have the short O sound as in /AHKS/.
Say these words: frog ox mop sock

If O is followed by an R, it can sound like this: horse order orange fork

Page 81. The letter O with a silent E sounds like the long O, /O/. The letters OA can sound like long O. And many other words have an /O/ sound.
Say these words: rope colt cold bone boat snow bowl toaster

Some other words with long O sounds are : go no so know

Page 82. The letter O followed by W or U sounds like this: /OU/.
Say these words: cow towel flower owl crown mountain mouth cloud house mouse

Page 83. The letters OY and OI sound like this: /OY/.
Say these words: boy oyster toys joint coin soil point

The letters OO often sound like this: /U/.
Say these words: hood foot hook hoof

Track 16, pages 86 and 89.

Page 86. The letter P at the beginning of a word sounds like this: /PUH/.
Say these words: paint pan pig peanuts pear push piano plant pie plate peas pull point pizza pumpkin paper pen pencil pants

Page 89. The letter Q almost always is followed by the letter U. Their sound is /KWUH/.
Say these words: quilt square quarter queen equator question mark squirrel aquarium quart equals quack

Track 17, page 90.

Page 90. The letter R at the beginning of a word sounds like this: /RRR/.
Say these words: ride rock road robot rat read rabbit rose rocket rain ring run roof ruler river radio

Track 18, page 94.

Page 94. The letter S sounds like this at the beginning of a word: /SSS/.
Say these words: sleep sky sun spoon star socks snake scissors south spider subtraction smell sing snail six seven swim square smoke

Track 19, page 100.

Page 100. The sound of the letter T at the beginning of a word is /TUH/.
Say these words: tie television TV triangle tail tiger table teeth T-shirt toe turtle two ten twenty twelve talk tomato toaster toast tree truck train

Track 20, pages 106, 108, 109.

Page 106. The letter U at the beginning of a word is usually pronounced /UH/.
Say these words: umbrella underwear unzip umpire unhappy up underwater underground upside down duck undershirt untied shoelace

Page 108. The short U can occur at the beginning or in the middle of a word.
Say these words: umbrella sun duck cup

U followed by the letter R sounds like this: /ERRR/.
Say these words: turtle church purse turkey

Page 109. The long U sound has many spellings. Here are some: U followed by E as in mule, UE as in glue, UI as in fruit, OO as in root, and EW as in screw.
Say these words: mule glue root tooth screw spoon tube fruit

Track 21, page 110.

Page 110. The letter V sounds like this: /VVVV/.
Say these words that begin with V: volcano violin vest van vegetables valley village valentine vowels vase vacuum cleaner vine

Track 22, page 114.

Page 114. The letter W at the beginning of a word sounds like this: /WUH/ .
Say these words: web   west   wasp   wing   watch   wake up   window   woman   wolf   wait   wall   water   wash   wave   walk

But it can sound like an R if R follows it, for example /RAYT/ .
Say these words: write   wrote   written   writing

Track 23, page 118.

Page 118. The letter X is really two sounds /KUH/ and /SUH/ said quickly.
Say these X words: x-ray   six   sixty   fox   exit   taxi   ax   sixteen   exercise   hexagon   box   saxophone   ox

Track 24, pages 120 and 122.

Page 120. The letter Y's sound is /YUH/.
Say these words: yolk   yoga   yogurt   yarn   yell   yam   yawn   yak   yard   yo-yo

Page 122. The letter Y can also sound like a vowel. For example /AY/, /EE/, and /I/ .
Say these words: sky   frying pan   cry   baby   happy   sunny   bicycle   cylinder   cymbals

Track 25, pages 123 and 124.

Page 123. The letter Z at the beginning of a word sounds like this: /ZZZZ/.
Say these words: zebra   zoo   zigzag   zucchini   zip code   zipper   zero

Page 124. The letter Z can be in the middle of a word. Sometimes there are two Zs.

Activities Answer Key

A Activities

p. 2: 2 acrobat, 3 arm, 4 alligator

p. 3: 2 no, 3 no, 4 yes, 5 no, 6 yes, b alligator, c arm

p. 4: 2 apple, 3 arm, 4 star, 5 apple, 6 car

p. 5: 2 tail, 3 paint, 4 day, 5 rain, 6 cake

p. 6: 2 saw, 3 saucer, 4 draw, 5 walk, 6 salt

p. 7: **short a:** pan, rat, man, hat. **long a:** cake, tape, rain, tray, paint. **ar:** arm, card, jar, star. **aw:** saw ball, walk, saucer, claw, car

p. 8: 2 cow, 3 dog, 4 elephant, 5 giraffe, 6 horse, 7 lion, 8 monkey, 9 octopus, 10 pig, 11 shark, 12 tiger

p. 9: 3 front seat, 4 gas cap, 5 headlight, 6 hood, 7 license plate, 8 roof, 9 steering wheel, 10 tire, 11 trunk, 12 wheel, 13 windshield, 14 wiper

B Activities

p.10: 2 branch, 3 bus, 4 bike

p.11: 2 no, 3 no, 4 yes, 5 no, 6 yes, b little, c little

p.12: 2 blanket, 3 brush, 4 branch, 5 blouse, 6 broom

C Activities

p.14: 2 cat, 3 crayon, 4 carrot

p.15: Answers will vary.

p.16: 2 chicken, 3 face, 4 bicycle, 5 cheese, 6 celery

p.17: b purple, c orange

p.18: twenty-four, seventy, eighty-five, thirty- three, eleven, two hundred, one hundred nine

p.19: Answers will vary.

p.20: Answers will vary.

p.21: Answers will vary.

D Activities

p. 22: 2 dollar, 3 dress, 4 diamond

p. 23: Answers will vary.

p. 24: 2 drink, 3 belt, 4 gift, 5 diamond, 6 jump

p. 25: 2 Monday, 3 Friday, 4 Thursday, 5 Tuesday, 6 Sunday, 7 Saturday

E Activities

p. 26: 2 exit, 3 elevator, 4 engine

p. 27: 2 yes, 3 no, 4 yes, 5 no, 6 no; b elbow, c envelope

p. 28: 2 bell, 3 pen, 4 fern, 5 water, 6 ruler

p. 29: 2 eat, 3 see, 4 tree, 5 ear, 6 teeth

p. 30: Answers will vary.

p. 31: Answers will vary.

F Activities

p. 32: 2 flower, 3 flute, 4 fruit

p. 33: 2 falling, 3 catching, 4 drawing, 5 driving, 6 eating

p. 34: 2 alphabet, 3 phone, 4 elephant, 5 laugh, 6 alphabet

p. 35: Answers will vary.

p. 36: Answers will vary.

p. 37: **avocado:** green. **banana:** green, yellow. **cherries:** red, purple. *grapes:* red, green, purple. **lemon:** yellow. **grapefruit:** yellow. **pear:** green, yellow. **strawberry:** red

p. 38: 1 eyes, 2 mouth, 3-4 answers will vary

p. 39: Answers will vary.

G Activities

p. 40: 2 grapes, 3 glasses, 4 grass

p. 41: 2 going, 3 growing, 4 getting off, 5 eating, 6 drinking

p. 42: 2 cabbage, 3 ring, 4 giant, 5 sing, 6 page

p. 43: Answers will vary.

H Activities

p. 44: 2 hill, 3 hair, 4 hen

p. 45: 2 have, 3 have, 4 has, 5 have, 6 have

p. 46: 2 shark, 3 thumb, 4 whale, 5 wheel, 6 whistle

p. 47: Answers will vary.

p. 49: Answers will vary.

I Activities

p. 50: 2 insect, 3 iguana, 4 igloo

p. 51: 2 Is he, 3 Are they, 4 Are you, 5 Am I, 6 Is it

p. 52: 2 skirt, 3 bird, 4 fish, 5 sit, 6 shirt

p. 53: 2 bike, 3 fly, 4 thigh, 5 drive, 6 sky

p. 54: Answers will vary.

p. 55: 1 6 parts. 2 1 thorax, 2 wings, 1 abdomen, 1 head, 2 antennae. 2 butterfly /moth/ dragonfly. 3 bee. 4 wasp / bee. 5 dragonfly

J Activities

p. 56: 2 jet, 3 jump, 4 jam / jelly

p. 57: 2 No, she isn't, 3 Yes, he is, 4 No, she isn't, 5 Yes, he is, 6 Yes, she is

p. 58: 2 cupcake, 3 snowman, 4 sunflower, 5 birdhouse, 6 bathtub

p. 59: 2 pilot, 3 teacher, 4 doctor, 5 newscaster, 6 firefighter, 7 Answers will vary.

K Activities

p. 60: 2 ketchup, 3 kangaroo, 4 kitten

p. 61: 2 No, we are not. 3 Yes. I am. 4. No, they are not. 5 No, we are not. 6 Yes, she is.

p. 62: 2 clock, 3 jacket, 4 chicken, 5 kick, 6 duck

p. 63: Answers will vary.

L Activities

p. 64: 2 looking at, 3 light, 4 love

p. 65: 2 sing, 3 kick, 4 get on, 5 eat, 6 go

p. 66: 2 paddle, 3 petal, 4 bottle 5 handle, 6 candle

p. 67: 2 at the top / on the right, 3 at the bottom /on the right, 4 at the bottom / on the left, 5 on the right

A to Z Picture Activities: Phonics and Vocabulary for Emerging Readers

M Activities

p. 68: 2 music / monkey, 3 mouth / moon, 4 mug

p. 69: 2 meet, 3 mop, 4 listen, 5 sit, 6 drive

p. 70: 2 climb, 3 comb, 4 lamb, 5 thumb, 6 crumb

p. 71: Answers will vary.

N Activities

p. 72: Answers will vary.

p. 73: 2 50, 3 20, 4 2, 5 2

p. 74: 2 net, 3 necklace, 4 night

p. 75: 2 never, 3 sometimes, 4 always, 5 never, 6 sometimes

p. 76: 2 gnome, 3 knife, 4 knock, 5 knot, 6 design

p. 77: 2 3, 3 50, 4 25, 5 even

O Activities

p. 78: 2 octagon, 3 October, 4 office

p. 79: 2 big, 3 long, 4 odd, 5 high, 6 happy

p. 80: 2 sock, 3 fork, 4 order, 5 orange, 6 ox

p. 81: 2 snow, 3 boat, 4 rope, 5 colt, 6 bone

p. 82: 2 mountain, 3 mouse, 4 owl, 5 mouth, 6 house

p. 83: 2 hood, 3 toys, 4 joint, 5 soil, 6 foot

p. 84: 11th eleventh, 5th fifth, 1st first, 20th twentieth, 100th one hundredth, 3rd third, 8th eighth

p. 85: 2 square, 3 octagon, 4 oval, 5 pentagon, 6 triangle, 7 hexagon

P Activities

p. 86: 2 pen, 3 plant, 4 pizza

p. 87: 2 pulled, 3 pointed, 4 painted, 5 listened, 6 moved

p. 88: 2 pennies, 2 dishes, 2 pans, 2 foxes, 2 glasses

Q Activities

p. 89: 2 queen, 3 aquarium, 4 quart, 5 equator, 6 square

R Activities

p. 90: 2 rabbit, 3 radio, 4 rocket

p. 91: 2 read, 3 meet, 4 ride, 5 cook, 6 go

p. 92: b 8, c 32, d 2

p. 93: 2 taller- tallest, 3 older- oldest, 4 newer–newest, 5 faster- fastest, 6 slower- slowest, 7 softer- softest, 8 harder- hardest

S Activities

p. 94: 2 sing, 3 seven, 4 spider

p. 95: 2 sleep, 3 see, 4 sit, 5 sing, 6 stop

p. 96: 2 right, 3 pair, 4 meet, 5 not, 6 write

p. 97: 2 spring, summer, thunderstorm, fall / autumn

p. 98: 2 soccer, 3 skiing, 4 basketball, 5 baseball, 6 football

p. 99: Answers will vary.

T Activities

p. 100: 2 tiger, 3 TV, 4 triangle

p. 101: 2 false, 3 true, 4 false, 5 false, 6 false, 7 true, 8 false, 9 true, 10 false, 11 false, 12 true

p. 102: 2 ear, 3 ear, 4 fly, 5 bow, 6 bat, 7 fly, 8 bow

p. 103: 2 train, 3 boat, 4 subway, 5 car / van, 6 plane, 7 truck / train, 8 ambulance

p. 104: 2 eight o'clock, 3 nine twenty, 4 five fifteen, 5 eleven thirty-five, 6 seven ten

p. 105: 2 hammer, 3 saw, 4 rake, 5 scissors, 6 pliers

U Activities

p. 106: 2 umpire, 3 upside down, 4 up

p. 107: 2 unzip / zip, 3 underground, 4 untied, 5 unhappy, 6 underwater

p. 108: 2 turkey, 3 cup, 4 sun, 5 turtle, 6 purse

p. 109: 2 fruit, 3 spoon, 4 tube, 5 root, 6 screw

V Activities

p. 110: 2 vegetable, 3 violin, 4 vase

p. 111: 2 swimming, 3 walking, 4 reading, 5 talking, 6 listening, 7 sleeping, 8 kissing

p. 112: 2 holding, 3 sitting, 4 painting, 5 riding, 6 laughing, 7 smelling, 8 mopping

p. 113: **broccoli:** green. **carrot:** orange. **corn:** yellow, purple, white. **lettuce:** green. **onion:** yellow, purple, white. **pepper:** red, green, yellow, orange. **potato:** red, orange, white. **squash:** green, yellow, orange, white

W Activities

p. 114: 2 wait, 3 window, 4 wolf

p. 115: 2 will write, 3 will wake up, 4 will wash, 5 will watch, 6 will wait

p. 116: 2 verb, 3 adjective, 4 adverb, 5 noun, 6 preposition, 7 article

p. 117: 2 woman / girl, 3 water, 4 3:00, 5 flour, 6 December, 7 Answers will vary.

X Activities

p. 118: 2 box, 3 exercise, 4 hexagon

p. 119: 2 Will he go, 3 Will we wake up, 4 Will she wait, 5 Will you read, 6 Will they wash

Y Activities

p. 120: 2 yolk, 3 yawn, 4 yam

p. 121: 2 no, 3 yes, 4 no, 5 no, 6 yes, 7 no, 8 no, 9 no, 10 no, 11 yes, 12 yes

p. 122: 2 bicycle, 3 baby, 4 sky, 5 frying pan, 6 cymbals

Z Activities

p. 123: 2 zipper, 3 zoo, 4 zucchini

p. 124: 2 Answers will vary

Index of Illustrated Words

The words in phonetic script are available at www.ProLinguaAssociates.com under *A to Z Picture Activities*.

earphones 20
earrings 19
Easter 49
eat 29, 31
egg 26, 28, 31, 72
eggplant 113
eight 18
eighteen 18
eighth 84
eighty 18
elbow 13, 26
electric drill 105
elephant 8, 26, 34
elevator 26
eleven 26, 18
eleventh 84
end table 48
engine 26
enter 26
envelope 26
equals 2, 73, 77, 89
equator 89
eraser 20
even numbers 77
exercise 26, 118
exit 26, 118
eye 38, 96
eye brow 38
eye lashes 38
face 38
fall (v) 6, 32
fall (n) 97
family 35
father 35
faucet 63
February 49
feelings 39
fern 28
fever 54
fifteen 18, 32
fifth 84
fifty 18
fin 32
finger 13
fire 32
firefighter 59
first 84
fish 30, 32, 52, 99
five 18, 32
flag 20, 32
flame 32
floor 20, 32
flour 43, 96
flower 32, 82, 96
flute 32, 71

fly 32, 53, 55, 102
foot 13, 32, 83, 92
football 58, 98
forehead 38
fork 30, 32, 80
forty 18
four 18
fourteen 18
fourth 84
fox 88, 118
fraction 77
freezer 63
Friday 25
frog 32, 80
front seat 9
fruit 32, 37, 109
fry 53
frying pan 63, 122
furnace 48
gallon 92
game 40
garden 40
gas 40
gas cap 9
gate 40
get off 40
get on 40
giant 42
gift 24, 40
giraffe 8, 42
girl 40, 52
give 40
glad 39
glass 30, 40
glasses 40
globe 21
glove 40
glue 109
gnome 76
go 40
goat 40
golf 98
good-bye 40
gorilla 40
grains 43
grams 92
grandfather 35
grandmother 35
grapefruit 37
grapes 37, 40
grass 40
greater than 77
green beans 30
green onions 99
groceries 43

grocery cart 43
grocery store 67
grow 40
guitar 71
gum 40
hair 13, 38, 44
hairdresser 59
half dollar 73
Halloween 49
ham 72
hamburger 31, 72
hammer 44, 105
hand 13, 44
handle 44, 66
hanger 42
Hanukkah 25, 49
happy 39, 122
harmonica 71
harp 71
hat 4, 7,19. 44
head 13, 44, 55
headache 54
headlight 9
hear 29, 44
heart 49
hen 28, 44
hexagon 85, 118
high heels 19
hill 44
hip 13
hit 44
hold 44
hole 44
honey 43
hood 9, 48, 83
hoof 83
hook 83
hop 44
horse 8, 44, 80
hot dog 44, 72
house 44, 47, 82
hug 44
hundred 18, 44
hundredth 84
husband 35
I 96
ice 53
ice cream 30, 72
igloo 50
iguana 50
ill 50
illness 54
inch 50, 52, 92
index finger 50
injury 54

ink 50
insect 50, 55
invitation 50
jack-o-lantern 49
jacket 19, 56, 62
jam 56
jar 4, 7, 56
jeans 56
jelly 56
jellyfish 58
jet 56
jewelry 56
jigsaw puzzle 56
jog 56
joint 83
juice 30, 31
jump 24, 56
kangaroo 60
kayak 60
kayak paddle 60
ketchup 43,60
key 60
kick 60, 62
kilometer 92
kilogram 92
king 60
kiss 52, 60
kitchen 47, 63
kite 60
kitten 60
knee 13
kneel 76
knife 30, 76
knob 76
knock 76
knot 76, 96
Kwanza 49
lamb 70
lamp 48, 64
laugh 34, 64
LCD projector 21
leaf 64
leave 64
left 67
leg 13, 55, 64
lemon 37, 64
length 92
less than 77
letter 64
lettuce 99, 113
library 67
license plate 9
lift 64
light 53, 64
lighthouse 58

limb 70
lime 37
line 64
lion 8, 64
lip 38, 64
liquids 92
list 24
listen 64
liters 92
little 11
living room 47
lizard 124
lobster 99
lock 62
longer, longest 93
look at 64
love 64
lunch 31
mad 39
main dishes 30
man 4, 7, 68
map 4, 7, 20, 68
March 49
marker 21
math 73, 77
math operations 77
math symbols 77
math terms 77
May 5
measurements 92
measuring cup 63
measuring spoons 63
meat 72, 96
mechanic 59
medal 66
medication 54
medicine 54
meet 68, 96
melon 68
menorah 49
microwave 63
mile 92
milk 30, 31, 68, 72
million 18
minus 77
minute 104
mirror 48, 68
mixer 63
Monday 25
money 73
monkey 8, 68
month 49
moon 68
mop 68, 80
moth 46, 55
mother 35
mountain 68, 82

mouse 68, 82
mouth 13, 38, 68, 82
move 68
mug 68
mule 109
multiplication 77
multiplied by 77
museum 67
music 68
mustard 43
nail 74
napkin 30
near 44
neck 13, 74
necklace 19, 74
nephew 35
nest 74
net 74
never 75
newscaster 59
New Year's Eve 25
next to 32
nickel 73
niece 35
night 53, 74
nine 18, 74
nineteen 18, 74
ninety 18, 74
ninth 84
noodles 43
noon 104
north 74
nose 13, 38, 74
notebook 21
November 49, 74
number 18, 74, 77
nut 74
octagon 78, 85
October 49, 78
octopus 8, 78
odd numbers 77, 78
off 78
office 78
olives 78,
on 78
onion 113
open 116
operations 77
opposites 79
orange 37, 78, 80
orange juice 31
order 78, 80
ordinal numbers 84
ostrich 78
ounce 92
oval 85
oven 63

owl 82
ox 78, 80, 118
oyster 83, 99
paddle 66
page 42
paint 5, 7, 86
painting 48
pair 96
pajamas 19
pan 86
pancakes 31, 43
pants 19, 86
paper 21, 28, 86
parallelogram 85
park 67
parts of speech 116
pasta 43
peach 37
peanut butter 43
peanuts 86
pear 37, 86, 96
peas 86, 113
pen 21, 86
pencil 21, 86
pencil sharpener 20
penny 73
pentagon 85
pepper 30, 113
percent 77
petal 66
phone 34
piano 71, 86
pie 30, 86
pig 8, 86
pilot 59
pineapple 37
pint 92
pizza 31, 86, 124
plane 103
plant 86
plate 5, 30, 86
pliers 105
plum 37
plurals 88
plus 77
pocket 62
point 83, 86
police officer 59
pool 76
pork chop 72
poster 20
potato 30, 113
pound 93
pretzels 124
problem 77
product 77
pull 86

pumpkin 86, 88
purse 19, 108
push 86
puzzle 124
puzzled 39
quart 89, 92
quarter 73, 89
queen 89
question mark 89
quilt 89
quotient 77
rabbit 90
radio 90
rain 5, 7, 90
rainy 97
rake 105
raspberry 37
rat 7, 90
rattle 66
read 90
rectangle 85
refrigerator 48, 63
rice 30, 43
ride 90
right 67, 96
ring 42, 90
river 90
road 90
robot 90
rock 90
rocket 90
roof 9, 90
room 47
root 109
rope 81
rose 90
rug 48
ruler 21, 28, 90, 92
run 90
sad 39
salad 30, 31, 99
salt 6, 30, 43
sandwich 31
Saturday 25
sauce pan 63
saucer 6, 7
saw 6, 7, 105
saxophone 71, 118
scared 39
school 67
scientist 59
scissors 21, 94, 105
screw 109
screwdriver 105
seafood 99
season 97
second 84

see 29
sentence 116
seven 18, 94
seventeen 18
seventh 84
seventy 18
shapes 85
shark 8, 46
sheep 29
shelf 48
shirt 19, 52
shoes 19
shorts 19
shoulder 13
shovel 105
shower 48
shrimp 99
side dishes 30
sign 76
sing 42, 94
sink 48, 63
sister 35
sit 52, 94
six 18, 94, 118
sixteen 18, 118
sixth 84
sixty 18, 118
skiing 98
skirt 19, 52
sky 53, 94, 122
sleep 94
slow 116
smaller, smallest 93
smell 94
smoke 94
snail 94
snake 94
snow 81
snowman 58
snowy 97
soccer 98
socks 19, 62, 93, 94
sofa 48
soil 83
sometimes 75
son 35
song 42
sore throat 54
south 94
spaghetti 30
spider 94
spinach 99, 113
spoon 30, 94, 109
sports 98
sprained ankle 54
spring 97
square 85, 89

squash 113
squirrel 89
stairs 47
star 4, 7, 94
steak 30, 72
steering wheel 9
stethoscope 54
stitches 54
stomach ache 54
stop sign 76
St. Patrick's Day 49
stove 48, 63
strawberry 37
student 20
subtraction 77, 94
subway 103
sugar 43
suit 19
sum 77
summer 97
sun 94, 108
Sunday 25
sunny 97, 122
superlatives 93
surprised 39
sweater 19
swim 94
swimming pool 67
syringe 54
T-shirt 19, 100
table 20, 48, 100
taco 31
tail 5, 7, 100
talk 100
tape 5, 7
taxi 100, 118
teacher 20, 59
teeth 29, 38, 100
ten 100
tennis 98
tenth 84
Thanksgiving 49
thermometer 54
thigh 53
third 84
thirteen 18
thirty 18
thorax 55
thousand 18
three 18
thumb 13, 70
thunderstorm 97
Thursday 25
tie (n) 19
tie (v) 100
tiger 8, 100
time 104

times 77
tire 9
toast 100
toaster 81, 83, 100
toe 13, 100
toilet 48
tomato 37, 99, 100
tools 105
tooth 109
top 67
towel 82
toy s 83
track and field 98
train 100, 103
trapezoid 85, 124
trash can 20, 63
tray 5, 7
tree 29, 49, 100
triangle 85, 100
trombone 71
truck 100, 103
true 101
trumpet 71
trunk 9
tube 109
Tuesday 25
turkey 49, 108
turtle 100, 108
TV/television 48, 100
twelve 100
twenty 100
twice 84
two 100
umbrella 106, 108
umpire 106
uncle 35
undershirt 106
underground 106
underwater 106
underwear 106
unhappy 106
untied shoelace106
unzip 106
up 106
upside down 106
vacuum cleaner 110
valentine 49, 110
valley 110
van 103, 110
vase 110
vegetables 110, 113
verbs 111, 112
vest 19, 110
village 110
vine 110
violin 71, 110
volcano 110

vowels 110
wait 114
wake up 114
walk 6, 114, 116
wall 20, 114
wash 114
washing machine 48
wasp 55, 114
watch (n) 19
watch (v) 114
water 28, 48, 114
water heater 48
wave 114
weather 97
web 114
Wednesday 25
weight 92
west 114
whale 46
wheel 9, 46
wheelchair 54
whistle 46
whiteboard 20
whole number 77
wife 35
window 20, 114, 116
window curtains 48
windshield 9
windy 97
wing 55
winter 97
wiper 9
wizard 124
wolf 114
woman 114, 116
worried 39
wrist 13
write 96, 114
writing 20
x-ray 54, 118
xylophone 71
yak 120
yam 120
yard 92, 120
yarn 120
yawn 120
yell 120
yoga 120
yogurt 120
yolk 120
yo-yo 120
zebra 123
zero 123
zigzag 123
zip code 123
zipper 123
zoo 67, 123
zucchini 123

Other Pro Lingua Books of Interest

Superphonic Bingo: 15 photocopyable games following the presentation of sound-letter combinations in *From Sound to Sentence*. Each game has 8 different cards and two incomplete cards.

English Interplay: Surviving: An integrated skills text for absolute beginners. Lots of pair and small-group work. A variety of activities: exchanges, rituals, operations, games, rhymes. Includes grammar notes, pronunciation practice. Features 10 units focused on survival language. Separate **Teacher's Book** is available. Includes all the student material plus suggestions and instructions for the teacher and additional resource material.

From Sound to Sentence: This book combines a basic phonics approach with key sight words and leads the learner from one-syllable combinations of three vowels and four consonants through a comprehensive progression of the English sound-symbol system. After the first unit, the learner is reading short sentences such as "Dad did it." The final reading is, "We the people of the United States . . ." Three CDs are available.

Rhymes 'n Rhythms: Your students will enjoy the choral work in these 32 rhythmic rhymes that develop the student's ability to speak with English stress, rhythm, and intonation. A CD is also available for use with this photocopyable text.

Teaching North American English Pronunciation: There are two parts to this book. Part One, for the teacher, is a brief introduction to English phonology, including the suprasegmental system of stress, intonation, rhythm, and linking. Part Two is a collection of photocopyable handouts to be used with learners. Three CDs are available.

Pronunciation Activities: Vowels in Limericks: 16 comical limericks present the basic vowels of English. Each limerick is followed by a variety of pronunciation and sound-letter correspondence activities. Cassette or CD available.

The Read and Learn Series: Four separate, graded readers. In **Read 50,** the average passage is only 50 words long. The other books are **Read 75, Read 100,** and **Read 125.** Each reading passage is followed by brief exercises. A wide variety of topics and formats are included in the 160 passages in the four-book collection. CDs are available.

Where in the World: This integrated skills text takes the reader around the world to 30 fascinating places from Antarctica to Wyoming. The first group of places features very easy readings of 50-75 words in length. By the end of the journey at the National Mall, the readings average 140-175 words long. Each unit includes easy work on vocabulary, grammar, listening, and writing. Two basic CDs are available, a well as two CDs of dictations.

Pro Lingua Associates
PO Box 1348
Brattleboro, VT 05302

Orders: (800) 366-4775
FAX: (802) 257-5117
Email: Info@ProLinguaAssociates.com
Webstore: www.ProLinguaAssociates.com